Hello from 3050 AD!

by

Rev. Joseph Adam Pearson, Ph.D.

Copyright

Published by
Christ Evangelical Bible Institute
(SAN: 920-3753)
Dayton, Tennessee

Last edited on August 16, 2022

Dedication

This book is dedicated to the Lord Jesus Christ and all people who belong to him during the remainder of *the Pre-Millennium* as well as all people who belong to him throughout *the Millennium*.

For the sake of clarity, "the remainder of *the Pre-Millennium*" is the period of time left until the Second Advent/Second Coming of Jesus Christ (i.e., his return to Earth). And *the Millennium* is the 1,000 years of peace during which Jesus Christ reigns on Earth, beginning with his Second Advent.

Table of Contents

Foreword

In the literary world, an author is a pure writer when he or she writes for oneself and not for others. In the world of Christian metaphysics, an author is a pure writer when he or she writes only to please the God of the Holy Bible. In either case, a pure writer imposes constraints upon his or her own writing in terms of clarity and understandability, but a pure writer is unfettered by seeking to please a desired audience or to advance marketability and increase salability of one's own written work. Indeed, as a pure writer of Christian metaphysics, I have tried to make my written work on spiritual truth clear and understandable in order: (1) to please the Creator-God; and (2) to accurately express what I see so that I can evaluate my own faith-based belief system in order to discover if there are any flaws in it. If there are flaws in my ideas about Christian metaphysics, then there will be dissonance within my own spirit as I review my writing. To be sure, I would like others to read what I have written and learn from what I have written, but that is not my primary reason for writing. My primary reason is to please the Creator-God, who is our one true and only real Self. It is He who has called me to write about what I am able to see.

If I do not correct the flaws in my belief system by editing and refining my writing (which is really editing and refining my thinking), then I will not bring the highest praise to my Creator-God, and my writing will be of no real value and have no lasting benefit for others who may read it. Although I think that my written works may eventually become of interest to a number of people, I believe that the popular consumption of my works will occur only after I have left this world for the here-beyond — not because I have left but because some time is necessary in order for people to become aware of my written works.

Pure writing is time-consuming and requires significant focus to get it right. As a pure writer, I view the blank page as a canvas on which I need to paint edifying words that accurately express spiritual truth. Not only does good painting require great care in detailing and texturing — good writing also requires great care in detailing and texturing. A good painting often shows that it is good because of the enhanced dimensionality in its expressed views on life. Likewise, a good written work shows that it is good because of the enhanced dimensionality in its articulated views on life. A good painter revisits his or her work with a paint brush in order to add detailing and touch up what has already been painted. A good writer does the same with pen or keyboard in editing. A good painting requires some objectivity on the part of its painter. And a good written work requires the same on the part of its author. Stepping back from a painting permits the painter to attain some objectivity about one's own painting. Likewise, stepping back from a written work — that is, allowing some time to pass before rereading it — permits the author to attain some objectivity about one's own written work.

Pure writing is never really finished. The pure writer can revisit his or her written work over decades to make necessary changes. Necessary changes are required because, as the author lives, the author grows in depth of character and his or her views become sharper and have more textured layers to them. It is impossible to live as a human being and not grow unless one is on a path to destruction. If we are not on a path to destruction, experience and an inquiring mind require us to grow.

If you, the reader or listener, have discovered this written work, I ask that you give the ideas within it some time to distill in your own thinking before you pass final judgment on them. Please allow this work's intended meanings to sink in as you cogitate on them. Indeed, I even hope that you might eventually be able to savor some of its intended meanings.

I have written only what I believe to be true. For today, I have expressed my ideas as clearly and precisely as I can. I hope my ideas impinge upon your consciousness a new way of looking at the topics covered in this book. Perhaps you will be able to incorporate some of this book's ideas into your own way of looking at life — if you find them of value.

Until some other time and place, much love from me to you in the name of Jesus Christ, the *only-begotten* Son of the Creator-God, the God of the Holy Bible!

Rev. Joseph Adam Pearson, Ph.D.

Notes

As used in this book, *KJV* is an abbreviation for the public domain *King James Version* of the Holy Bible. To ensure their accuracy throughout this book, all paraphrases of the public domain *King James Version* of the Holy Bible were finalized only after first checking: (1) the Masoretic Hebrew text of the Tanakh (the Jewish Bible) for accuracy of passages from the *KJV Old Testament;* and (2) the earliest Greek text extant for accuracy of passages from the *KJV New Testament.* Additionally, to enhance readability of the public domain *KJV* text, the present author has changed words like *hath, thou,* and *ye* to their modern equivalents.

Although God the Father (i.e., the *Lord God Almighty)* and God the Son (i.e., the *Lord Jesus Christ)* are consubstantially united in the Godhead along with God the Holy Spirit, in order to distinguish *God the Father* from *God the Son,* an upper case "H" is used for personal pronouns specifically referring to *God the Father (He, His,* and *Him)* and a lower case "h" is used for personal pronouns specifically referring to *God the Son (he, his,* and *him).*

Although the Creator-God does not possess a human gender, there are no apologies for the use of the male pronouns *He, His, and Him* when referring to the Lord God Almighty in this book for the following reason: In general, certain words in theology and philosophy are capitalized to show that they represent qualities and characteristics that transcend human understanding and experience. This includes the pronouns *He, His,* and *Him* and even the word *God* itself. *She* and *Her* are not used in this book when referring to the Creator-God because many people, if not most, have a tendency to confuse the use of female pronouns with advocating Wicca and other cults that worship the pagan Mother-Goddess — such as those religions devoted to Cybele, Aphrodite, Hecate, Artemis, Magna Mater, Ma, Anaitis, Astarte, or their modern counterparts.

Whenever the word *God* is used in this book (i.e., with an upper case "G"), the reader should assume that the word is referring to the God of the Holy Bible — who is the *Lord God Almighty* or *Yahweh* (YHWH), the one true and only real Creator-God.

For the sake of clarity, when the author of *Hello from 3050 AD!* uses the phrase *the present author* in this book, he is referring to himself and not to some other author or source.

Finally, it is important for the reader to understand that repetition, redundancy, and reiteration have been used by the present author in this book to help clarify novel terminology and difficult concepts (i.e., terminology and concepts new to the reader).

Key words and phrases for external word search purposes include: Christian metaphysics, divine metaphysics, eschatology, Millennium, mortality, immortality, corporeality, incorporeality, incarnate, discarnate, *astral gelatinous*™, theion, and reincarnation.

Before beginning with Chapter One, the author recommends that the reader first review definitions of important terms and phrases in the Glossary of this book (Appendix B).

Chapter One

Living in Eternity: Part One

I am writing to you from 3050 AD. Actually, I am writing to you from the "now" of eternity, but I wanted you — the reader or listener — to be able to understand *when* I am writing to you relative to your own *Biblical time*. For the sake of clarity, *Biblical time* is the specific seven-thousand year period of chronological time covered by the Holy Bible from the Adamic Fall to the creation of "a new heaven and a new earth" (Revelation 21:1 KJV).

Basically, the Holy Bible covers seven thousand years that are divided into three periods: (1) four thousand years from the time of the Fall of Adam and Eve to the birth of Christ Jesus; (2) two thousand years from the first advent of Christ Jesus to the second advent of Christ Jesus (i.e., from his physical birth to his bodily return two millennia later); and (3) one thousand years (i.e., *the Millennium* during which Christ Jesus reigns on Earth) from his bodily return to the creation of "a new heaven and a new earth."

Eternity has neither a beginning nor an ending. Events in eternity are not chronological according to the relative space-time that you — the reader or listener — experience in corporeality. *For example,* when Enoch, Abraham, Moses, and Elijah transitioned from temporality to eternity, Enoch did not transition into a time earlier in eternity than Abraham, Moses, or Elijah even though Enoch lived on Earth earlier than the other three. And, on the other hand, when Elijah transitioned from temporality to eternity, Elijah did not transition into a time later in eternity than Enoch, Abraham, and Moses even though Elijah lived on Earth later than the other three. Enoch, Abraham, Moses, and Elijah all met, and meet, in eternity (yes, *meet* in the *eternal now* sense) because each individual consciousness in eternity intersects with all others at the metaphysical origin of eternity. *(The metaphysical origin of eternity* is the one true and only real Creator-God, the God of the Holy Bible.)

Although eternity may be a place (i.e., a locus or location), it is not just a place because eternity is always, first and foremost, a *state of being;* and every *state of being* always precedes in existence the place where that *state of being* is located. And just as one molecule of water is virtually indistinguishable from all other molecules of water in an ocean, so is one phase of absolute time in eternity virtually indistinguishable from all other phases of absolute time in eternity.

You might have learned that eternity is circular. Although it would be more accurate figuratively to state that eternity is spherical (see Figure One in Chapter Four), eternity is circular in the sense that it is never-ending. Eternity is neither linear nor curvilinear. Although chronological time — or relative space-time — in the physical universe is curvilinear (somewhat like a coiled spring), it is not curved in the same sense that eternity is circular. Chronological time always has a start point and an end point; it always has a beginning and an ending. To be sure, there are multiple start points and multiple end points in the skeins of chronological time but start points and end points (as you know them) do not exist in the absolute time of eternity.

Eternity has no beginning and no ending. In your corporeal condition of mortal being, it is difficult for you to grasp the concept of eternity. However, there are numerous moments and instances during your lifetime on Earth when you can catch glimpses of eternity — that is, have insights concerning it: (1) You can catch glimpses of eternity when you relive certain experiences that you have had. *For example,* when you mentally relive intensely pleasant or intensely unpleasant experiences from your past, you grasp their timelessness because they are indelible in your consciousness, and you relive them as if they are current events. (2) You can catch glimpses of eternity when you use your imagination in dreams during sleep (especially during rapid eye movement sleep). During such states of dreaming, you are not constrained by chronological time. What you experience during such states of dreaming reflects eternity more than it reflects chronological time. In your dreams, you appear in one place and reappear somewhere else instantly. Through dreams, you observe beyond the veil of chronological time. (3) You can catch glimpses of eternity in the spiritual truths that you learn. The spiritual truths learned during your sojourn in corporeality are timeless and remain with you not only throughout your entire human life but also throughout eternity. Spiritual truths are eternal and ever-abiding within you even though all of them may not be at the forefront of your consciousness while you are on Earth. (4) You can catch glimpses of eternity when you praise the Creator-God in gratitude or pray to the Creator-God in humility. In praise and prayer, you move into the realm of eternity, where time as you know it ceases to exist. In praise and prayer, you come to understand your residence in eternity regardless of where you are in *the whole Universe.* (For the sake of clarity, *the whole Universe,* as used in this communication, includes everything that exists physically as well as everything that exists spiritually. Additional clarifications about *the whole Universe* will be presented in following chapters.) Finally, (5) you can catch glimpses of eternity as a gift from the Creator-God when you study the heavenly visions recorded in the Holy Bible by others — like the Prophet Ezekiel, the Prophet Isaiah, and the Apostle John.

When my soul was in corporeality during my last sojourn (i.e., my final incarnation) on Earth, I regularly moved into and out of eternity in the recognition of the truth that all thoughts are things and all things are thoughts. (Take the time to read about how you can reconcile reincarnation with the Holy Bible in Appendix A of this book.) In other words, I realized that all ideas and concepts are made of an essential, albeit incorporeal, substance and, conversely, that all material objects represent the tangibility of ideas, concepts, and constructs. It was in this realization that I especially experienced eternity. In truth, I walked between two worlds during my entire life when I was last on Earth.

When I last lived in corporeality, my legal name was *Joseph Adam Pearson*. When I entered eternity fully, completely, and permanently, my new name was revealed to me. What I am called by the Creator-God in eternity is something that only our Creator-God and I can know because it is sacred, intimate, and personal between the two of us. Others in eternity know me by an additional heavenly name but not by the sacred, personal, and intimate name that my Creator calls me. Lest you think that I am trying to place myself above others, please know that each saved person in eternity has a name that only our Creator-God and the individual person know because our Creator-God has designed, designated, and deigned a specific name for each created being who has been fully restored to eternity. Just as my God-given name in eternity is too sacred, personal, and intimate for you to know, so is your God-given name in eternity too sacred, personal, and intimate for me to know. Although I am not able to share this sacred, personal, and intimate name with you, I can tell you that it represents: (1) the sum total of my inner character, my outward personality, and all activities I attempted on behalf of our Creator-God while I was on Earth as well as (2) my unique relationship to the Creator-God (which, although unique, is no more unique than your relationship to Him). It also represents in what capacity I serve the Creator-God now — but more about that later in this communication. (God's Holy Spirit teaches in Revelation 19:12 that even Christ Jesus has one name that no one else knows or can know.)

Like all other souls, I was created in eternity, which would be *eons ago* by your reckoning. All souls were created at the same instant in eternity through the same vocalization, articulation, and actualization of the Creator-God. Because souls were *created,* every soul has a beginning. However, our common beginning cannot be understood in terms of chronological time because all souls were created *in eternity*. It may sound strange to you, but, once we were created, it was as if we always *were* (just as we always *are* and always *will be*). Because we all live, move, and have our being in eternity, it is even impossible for us now to imagine ourselves *not being. For example,* though I live in eternity, I cannot think back to a time when I was *not* (i.e., when I did not exist) or did not have consciousness. This is so, in part, because I always existed as an idea in the Supraconsciousness of our Creator-God before I was created. (If you try to think of a time when you did not exist, you, too, will not be able to imagine it.) In that way, I always existed just as you always existed. However, there was an instant in eternity when each one of us was *pushed into being* from idea status to a personal state of volitional self-awareness; it was then that we were *vocalized, articulated,* and *actualized* individually, collectively, and corporately — all at once by the divine Logos, or spoken Word, of God. Once created, souls cannot *think back,* or remember, when they did not exist. It is this simple: As soon as we were brought forth into being, we were *joined* in eternity to eternity.

Once souls were created by God, they cannot ever become *uncreated*. In other words, all souls will continue throughout eternity without ever stopping because all souls were created to be eternal. Just as you (the reader or listener) cannot take back a sincere kiss of friendship from a friend who has become unfaithful to your relationship, so also our Creator-God cannot undo His gift of granting eternity to each volitional and self-aware created being. Although "cannot" might seem like hyperbole concerning the omnipotent Creator-God, part of His gift of eternal life to newly-created beings was that He would never take the gift back. He imposed that constraint on Himself before He created us. This is what makes the gift of eternal life such a remarkable gift. We might destroy *the gift of being* given to us personally, but God still will not take it back. (Hence comes the notion of true freedom but only with responsibility.)

As *Joseph Adam Pearson,* I was born in 1947 AD and my soul was permanently restored to eternity when I died during the third year of the seven-year Tribulation. When the saved in Christ die, they do not "enter into their rest" in the way that certain religious people might think. Yes, those who permanently enter into eternity rest from the work that they were given to do while they were each in a human body, but they do not cease from being active when they are in eternity. We continue to remain active in eternity because we continue to do the work of our Creator-God. While in eternity, we may interact with human beings in their chronological time (i.e., during their own individual lifetimes), but we are still working and planning from the standpoint of eternity and not from the standpoint of temporality. Working and planning from the standpoint of eternity gives us a whole different perspective concerning what needs to be accomplished in the temporal world.

My time of death preceded the return of Christ Jesus to Earth for his millennial reign of peace on Earth. Many of my contemporaries were murdered for their Christian commitment during *the Tribulation* (i.e., the seven years immediately before Christ Jesus returned to Earth). At the time of my death, I was also martyred for my Christian commitment. I was just one of many to be martyred before Christ Jesus returned. For the sake of clarification (for those of you who might be uncertain), Christ Jesus only returns once. Therefore, what many of you have come to call *the Rapture* occurs toward the end of *the Tribulation* at the time that Christ Jesus returns. There is only one *Parousia* for Christ Jesus. (*Parousia* is a New Testament Greek word that means "arrival.") Thus, Christians live through *the Tribulation* — unless, of course, they are murdered, die in an accident, or die from natural causes during *the Tribulation*.

The following section is a *roundabout*. *Roundabouts* in this book are used to replace footnotes because most readers tend to think that footnotes are inconsequential to the main body of a written work and, for that reason, refrain from reading them. Each *roundabout* in this book is a detour that offers clarification and eventually brings the reader back to the main discourse. Each *roundabout* is as important to the entire discussion as the other sections in this book.

Roundabout Number One

At this juncture, it is important for me to take a detour and discuss the *saved dead* and the *unsaved dead* relative to chronological time.

All people in Christ Jesus — that is, all *saved people* — who lived before or at the time of his return (i.e., his *Parousia*) ended up ruling jointly with him during the thousand years that he ruled on Earth. This included: (1) all martyred and non-martyred saved people who had died before he returned (i.e., *the saved dead*) as well as (2) all living saved people whose bodies were raptured, or *translated* into eternity, at the time of his return. The only difference between the saved dead who were martyred and the saved dead not martyred is that: (1) those who had been martyred for their commitment to Christ Jesus during the time of *the Tribulation* ruled jointly with him *from Earth* during *the Millennium* (see Revelation 20:4); but (2) those who had not been martyred ruled jointly with him *from Heaven* in a place referred to in the Holy Bible as *New Jerusalem* (Revelation 3:12 and 21:2).

Throughout church history, many students of the Holy Bible were confused about many things that they read concerning *the dead*. Relevant to the topic of this *roundabout* is their recurring failure to understand exactly who "the dead" are in different Biblical contexts:

(1) To whom is "the dead" referring in 1 Thessalonians 4:13-16?

> {13} But I would not have you ignorant, brothers and sisters, concerning those who are asleep in Jesus, that you sorrow not, even as others who have no hope. {14} For if we believe that Jesus died and rose again, even so those also who sleep in Jesus will God bring with him. {15} For this we say to you by the word of the Lord, that we who are alive and remain at the return of the Lord shall not precede those who are already asleep in Jesus. {16} For the Lord himself shall descend from Heaven with a shout, with the voice of the archangel, and with the trumpet of God: and *the dead in Christ* [those who "sleep in Jesus"] shall rise first.
>
> *1 Thessalonians 4:13-16 KJV Paraphrase*

In 1 Thessalonians 4:16, *the dead in Christ* is referring to the saved dead whose souls have already gone on to be with the Lord in *Paradise,* or Heaven, at the precise moment of their deaths and were figuratively said to be *asleep in Jesus*. (Using the expression *asleep in Jesus* for saved people who had already died was a comfort to their loved ones who remained on Earth as well as a gentle reminder that they were not really dead.) The souls of these saved dead accompany Christ Jesus when he returns to Earth at his *Parousia* — at which time they themselves receive new somatic identities a nanosecond before the saved still on Earth receive their new somatic identities in their *translation* to eternity (i.e., in their *rapture, rising,* or *resurrection).* That "the dead in Christ shall rise first" is speaking of their dead bodies metaphysically *rising* when Christ Jesus returns with their souls. In other words, the bodies of the saved dead were resurrected, or *made anew,* at the time of Christ Jesus' return. Instantly, after the souls of the saved dead received their new somatic identities, those Christians who are still alive (i.e., those who still remain in their human bodies) are then caught up, or *gathered unto him,* at which time their bodies are *translated, raptured, raised,* or *resurrected* (all four terms are used synonymously here). Thus, those translated also (i.e., like the souls of those who had previously died in Christ) acquire new somatic identities. Regardless of where they are (i.e., in Heaven or on Earth), all saved in Christ Jesus receive new somatic identities at the time of his *Parousia,* which is at the beginning of *the Millennium.*

(2) To whom is "the dead" referring in Revelation 20:4b-5?

> {4b} And I saw the souls of those who were beheaded for the witness of Jesus and for the word of God — those who had neither worshiped the beast nor his image [i.e., "image" here is referring to *the abomination of desolation,* or the specific idolatry, prophesied by: (a) the Prophet Daniel in Daniel 8:13, 11:31, and 12:11; (b) Christ Jesus in Matthew 24:15 and Mark 13:14; and (c) the Apostle John in Revelation 13:14-15] and had not received the beast's mark upon their foreheads or in their hands; and they lived and reigned with Christ for a thousand years. {5} But *the rest of the*

dead lived not again until the thousand years were finished. This is the first resurrection.

Revelation 20:4-5 KJV Paraphrase

"The souls of those who were beheaded" in Revelation 20:4 are Christians who were martyred during the Tribulation because they refused to serve the Islamic Allah as promoted by the final end-time Antichrist. Because of their testimony, these Tribulation saints served (i.e., "reigned") with Christ Jesus during *the Millennium* as part of the "first resurrection" (Revelation 20:5) and were not subject to God's White Throne Judgment nor eternal damnation in "the second death" (Revelation 20:6) at the end of *the Millennium*.

The specific phrase *the first resurrection* is only used twice in the Bible — in Revelation 20:5 and 20:6. In those two verses, *the first resurrection* refers to the raising from the dead of Christian saints martyred during the Tribulation. However, technically speaking, *the first resurrection,* or the first redemption of bodies, occurs during these four Biblical events in the following sequence: (1) the raising of dead saints immediately after the resurrection of Christ Jesus as a kind of firstfruits or prototypic event for future believers (Matthew 27:51-53); (2) the *translation* of the bodies of the saints of God who returned from Heaven with Christ Jesus at his Second Coming (1 Thessalonians 4:15-16); (3) the rapture, or *catching away,* of Christian believers at the time of Jesus Christ's Second Coming (1 Thessalonians 4:17) — the English word *rapture* and the Latin word *rapturo* translated from the Biblical Greek word *harpazo* [ἁρπάζω]; and, of course, (4) the raising from the dead of Christian saints martyred during the Tribulation (Revelation 20:5-6). In other words, souls in the four categories just mentioned are all part of *the first resurrection.*

Author's Note: "The rest of the dead" in Revelation 20:5 is not referring to any of the saved in Christ who died before *the*

Millennium began. Like the dying thief on the cross who confessed Christ (Luke 23:43), their souls went immediately to be with Christ Jesus in *Paradise* (Heaven) upon their deaths. Here, "the rest of the dead" is referring to those unsaved people who died during *the Tribulation* and, thus, had not yet been judged. Therefore, "the rest of the dead" in Revelation 20:5 are not only *unsaved* but also *unjudged*. It is these dead whose souls are in suspended animation, or spiritual hibernation, during *the Millennium*.

All unsaved people are judged at the end of *the Millennium* except for two people: (1) Mohammed (who is represented by the first "beast" in Revelation 13:1, 13:12, 13:14-15, and 13:17-18 and by "the beast" in Revelation 16:13, 19:20, and 20:10); and (2) the final end-time Antichrist (who is represented by the two-horned, second "beast" in Revelation 13:11 and by the "false prophet" in Revelation 16:13, 19:20, and 20:10). Except for (1) Mohammed and (2) the final end-time Antichrist — who were both thrown into *the Lake of Fire* (i.e., the place of eternal damnation and torment) when Christ Jesus returned at the beginning of *the Millennium* — no other unsaved person was judged before the Great White Throne Judgment (Revelation 20:11) at the end of *the Millennium*. (For proof that Mohammed is the first beast in Chapter Thirteen of Revelation, refer to Appendix C in this book.)

Again, all unsaved people will be judged at the end of *the Millennium* except for: (1) Mohammed and (2) the final end-time Antichrist, who were both judged at the beginning of *the Millennium*. In contrast, saved people *are never judged* relative to the salvation, or eternal redemption, of their souls, but saved people *are judged* at the end of *the Millennium* relative to the specific heavenly rewards they will each receive for their obedience to the Great Commission. It is important to emphasize that those who were saved at the time that they died before *the Millennium* have no need of judgment concerning the salvation, or eternal redemption, of their souls because they already have been washed clean of all of their iniquity and sin: The debts for their sins had already been paid by the shed blood of the *only-begotten* Son of God, Jesus Christ, at the time that his blood was shed during his crucifixion. Thus, the eternal redemption of saved people had already been sealed by the indwelling of the Creator-God's Holy Spirit within them at the exact moment that they believed on God's *only-begotten* Son. That is why saved people do not need to be judged at the end of *the Millennium* relative to the eternal redemption of their souls.

Remember, the God of the Holy Bible is the God of the living and not of the dead (Matthew 22:32; Mark 12:27; and Luke 20:38). No Christian was, is, or ever will be spiritually dead. Thus, for authentic Christians (i.e., truly saved people), there is no such thing as *soul sleep,* suspended animation, or spiritual hibernation. In fact, all people in past generations who *have walked* — as well as those in this current generation who *are walking* — with the God of the Holy Bible are alive eternally, including all Old Testament saints. Although New Testament saints are "dead to their sins" and, therefore, figuratively "dead with Christ," they are never spiritually dead. Their souls were never *asleep in Jesus* except in a figurative sense. All saints are always alive, possessing full awareness and volition, regardless of whether they are in a physical body or not — which is to say, in corporeality or in incorporeality. (For the sake of clarity, both *corporeality* and *incorporeality* are conditions, modes, or realms of being: *corporeality* is the incarnate condition, mode, or realm; and *incorporeality* is the discarnate condition, mode, or realm.)

Even people who are in between two sequential lifetimes (i.e., in between two separate incarnations on Earth) are not *asleep.* For them, a clock is not ticking before they enter into their next life. They simply: (1) wake up at the end of their first life to find their human bodies dead, (2) assess what went wrong and what went right during their immediate past lifetime, (3) communicate with the Creator-God concerning what they still need to learn and would like to accomplish in an additional lifetime, and, then, (4) *time travel* by skipping over an interval of chronological time in order to enter into a newly-developing human embryo for their next incarnation. (Such opportunities are extensions of God's mercy, grace, and justice.)

(3) To whom is "the dead" referring in Revelation 20:13?

> {a} And the sea gave up *the dead* which were in it; {b} and *Death* and *Hell* delivered up *the dead* which were in them: {c} and their souls were judged every person according to their works.
>
> *Revelation 20:13 KJV Paraphrase*

Saved souls were never: (1) in the *sea,* (2) in a state of death (except for their sojourn in the metaphysical state of mortality before they were saved), or (3) permanently assigned to *Hell* (also known as *Sheol* in Hebrew and *Hades* in Greek). Therefore, Revelation 20:13 is not referring to the souls of the saved dead but, instead, to the souls of the unsaved dead. Further, the souls of the saved dead would have no need to be judged based on their works or on any other criterion (except to receive their heavenly rewards) because, as previously stated, their souls had already been cleansed of all iniquity and sin by the shed blood of the *only-begotten* Son of God, Jesus Christ. Thus, again (similar to the reference in Revelation 20:5), the dead that are spoken of in Revelation 20:13 are not only *unsaved* but also *unjudged.*

As a side note, *the sea* referenced in Revelation 20:13 does not have a literal meaning but, instead, a metaphysical meaning: *the sea* refers to *the bottomless pit of the Abyss in Hades,* which *pit* is:

(1) the temporary abode of the eternally lost dead (i.e., the evil dead); and (2) the realm of existence for certain fallen angels and certain unclean spirits that had already been *cast out* of the earth plane of consciousness. In contrast, the unsaved dead who are in *Death* (i.e., the state of being also known as *mortality)* and levels and realms of *Hell* other than its *bottomless pit* are metaphysically intestate: They never made eternal provisions for their souls because they neither consciously accepted nor consciously rejected the Lord Jesus Christ as personal Savior. The phrase *metaphysically intestate* means that they were in a metaphysical state of *limbo* (i.e., uncertainty) preceding the Great White Throne Judgment at the end of *the Millennium*. Saved people, regardless of whether they are in corporeality or in incorporeality, were never in a metaphysical state of uncertainty. Why? After their salvation, their eternal redemption was always assured.

End of Roundabout Number One

>>>>><<<<<

Living in Eternity: Part Two

Because of my desires, interests, experiences, and developed skills and abilities when I last lived as a human being on Earth, I performed Creator-assigned responsibilities during *the Millennium* as a Christian educator — cooperatively, not competitively — with: (1) hundreds of thousands of others on Earth who also had been martyred and (2) millions of others in Heaven who had not been martyred. Regardless of whether we jointly ruled with Christ Jesus from Earth or from Heaven, during *the Millennium* all of us served in equally-important capacities (no one was higher or lower in importance, or superior or inferior, to anyone else).

During the entire *Millennium,* I taught Christian education with a special emphasis on Christian metaphysics to human beings who lived during that one thousand year period. In other words, I taught people who lived during that time of peace how to view reality through the lens of the supernatural in addition to the lens of the natural. I helped them to think metaphysically, spiritually, and supernaturally using constructs with which they were, at first, unfamiliar but in whose understanding and use they gradually gained confidence.

I was an incorporeal being throughout *the Millennium* just as I now remain an incorporeal being after *the Millennium* — which means that my somatic identity is not made of human flesh. To be sure, at the time of the return of Christ Jesus to Earth, I had been given a new somatic identity just a split second before the rapture, or translation to eternity, of those authentic Christians still living on Earth. (The phrase *authentic Christians* is intended to contrast true Christians with those who are *nominal,* or *secular, Christians* — such people not really *Christian* at all.) Those who were raptured, or translated to eternity, were also given new somatic identities. Although all of our individual somatic identities were similar to one another, they were distinguishable from one another in terms of: (1) individual subtle nuances in somatic form, shape, and size; (2) combinations and proportions of rainbow colors emanating from each person; and (3) the kinds of vestments that each individual wore.

During *the Millennium,* those of us in eternity each had gold and silver fibers of light running through our garments in different configurations. All who were martyred for their faith in Christ Jesus also had a red thread of light running through their vestments. (1) Jointly ruling with Christ Jesus *from Earth* (as opposed to jointly ruling with Christ Jesus *from Heaven*) and (2) the red thread of light just mentioned are the only characteristics that ever distinguished the martyred from the non-martyred during *the Millennium*. After *the Millennium,* there are no characteristics or markers that distinguish saved souls from one another except for the individual names given to us by our Creator-God.

The return of Christ Jesus to Earth was signaled by a huge, instantaneous flash of glorious light (i.e., divine Light, heavenly Glory, or living Fire) encircling the globe from East to West, starting and ending at the Mount of Olives in Jerusalem, Israel. It started and ended in Jerusalem because our Creator-God long ago decreed Jerusalem to be the spiritual navel of the Earth. And it started and ended at the Mount of Olives in Jerusalem because Christ Jesus declared that the Mount of Olives would be where he would again set foot on Earth.

Interacting with human beings from eternity during *the Millennium* required those of us in eternity, whose somatic identities are in an *astral gelatinous*™ condition, to appear as semi-solid and translucent to those still in *human flesh*. We could present ourselves at will to them. Our appearance as semi-solid was less unsettling to those in human flesh bodies even though we could appear and disappear at will (which took some getting used to by human observers). I specify *human flesh* here because *spiritual flesh* (i.e., *astral gelatinous*™ flesh) is eternally different from *human flesh*.

Roundabout Number Two

At this juncture, it is important to explain the phrase *astral gelatinous*™. The phrase *astral gelatinous*™ was originated by the present author and first copyrighted in 2011 in his work entitled

Divine Metaphysics of Human Anatomy (United States Copyright Office TXu001788674).

The phrase *astral gelatinous*™ describes a substance that predominantly has spiritual qualities somewhat similar to the created substance of unfallen angels. This substance may also take on physical qualities depending on the dimensionality in which it is found. *For example,* when some angels enter into the physical realm (i.e., *push* themselves into relative space-time), they voluntarily take on human form and appear to be human even though they did not originate from, or in, a biological life form. This is exemplified by the two angels who first visited Abraham and, later, Lot in the city of Sodom — which visitations are recorded in Chapters Eighteen and Nineteen of the Book of Genesis. At one time, certain angels even stepped into physicality in order to mate with human beings. This interaction is recorded in Genesis 6:1-4 as having taken place between "the sons of God" and "the daughters of men." The giant *nephilim* (or "fallen ones") mentioned in the Holy Bible were the offspring of these unnatural sexual liaisons. (The sexual liaisons were *unnatural* because they took place between immortals and mortals.) The Holy Bible is clear that the angels who mated with human beings were relegated to the *bottomless pit of the Abyss in Hades* to await the Creator-God's justified punishment for their transgressions (see verse 6 in the Epistle of Jude).

The unfallen creation that originally reflected God's complete image and perfect likeness was *astral gelatinous*™ in nature (i.e., *in essence*). As a result of the Adamic Fall, the *astral gelatinous*™ substance of immortal beings, originally created in the complete image and perfect likeness of God, manifested as living physical substance (i.e., protoplasm). Consequently, the various cells, tissues, organs, and organ systems of the modern human being appeared, becoming mere representations, vestiges, remnants, and "fossilized impressions" of what they used to be. From the standpoint of eternity, all of this occurred instantly. From the standpoint of temporality, all of this occurred over eons of chronological time.

As indicated earlier, at the return of Christ Jesus all joint heirs with him received their new somatic identities. These new somatic identities not only resembled the body of the ascended Christ Jesus but also were (and still are) composed of the original *astral gelatinous*™ form and substance immortal beings had before the Adamic Fall.

For the sake of clarity, gender and sexual identity do not exist in an *astral gelatinous*™ condition of being. Beneficial mental and emotional characteristics often associated with each gender and sexual identity on Earth are fused together for each being in Heaven. (In other words, there are no males, females, hermaphrodites, or intersexuals in Heaven.)

Author's Note: The present author uses the phrase *astral gelatinous*™ synonymously with these terms: *metacrystalline, supracrystalline, supraplasmic,* and *glorified.*

End of Roundabout Number Two

>>>>><<<<<

Living in Eternity: Part Three

When Christ Jesus returned to Earth at the end of *the Tribulation,* Satan and all fallen beings under his command were relegated to *the bottomless pit of the Abyss in Hades* for 1,000 years (i.e., throughout *the Millennium).* Immediately after their incarceration, there began a peace unequaled by any other peace on Earth preceding the return of Christ Jesus. For a period of seven years before the return of Christ Jesus, there were significant Earth changes that included:

earthquakes, volcanic activity, the shifting of magnetic poles, huge tidal waves, and major climate changes as well as massive typhoons, cyclones, and hurricanes. The Earth changes during those seven years were significant changes, and the shapes of continents were altered drastically: some existing lands disappeared forever and some new lands emerged dramatically. And not only had the Earth's magnetic poles shifted but also the tilt of the Earth in relation to the Sun was altered so that: (1) where it had once been warm, it became cold; and (2) where it had once been cold, it became warm. To be sure, billions of human beings had been killed during *the Tribulation* — not only from God's Wrath in massive geologic changes but also from God's Wrath manifested in pestilence, plague, human conflict (including nuclear warfare), and the harvesting (removal) of wicked people from the Earth by the angels of God. Wickedness in the world had exploded because of external evil influences on already-existing corporate greed, individual lust, famine, urban street crime, and international terrorism born of delusions associated with false religion, spiritual apostasy, and political demagoguery. Wickedness due to false religion, spiritual apostasy, and political demagoguery resulted in the deprivation, persecution, torture, and martyrdom of millions of Christians throughout the world during that seven year period of time.

Once Christ Jesus returned to Earth, Satan and all other evil beings no longer had access to human beings. Therefore, hostility throughout the world was immediately quelled. Additionally, there was peace between and among all human beings on Earth because of an outpouring of God's Holy Spirit on them, which outpouring was sustained until the end of *the Millennium* when World War IV erupted (known as the Battle of Gog and Magog in Revelation 20:8). Finally, there was peace throughout the world and all cataclysmic geological activity ceased when Christ Jesus returned. To be sure, the Wrath of God had been appeased during the Tribulation and the entire Earth was at peace throughout *the Millennium.*

During *the Millennium,* heaven and Earth still existed. In the previous sentence, "heaven" refers to the sky, the physical atmosphere, and the physically observable universe and not to the eternal place where Christians go when they die (i.e., *Heaven).* It was not until the end of *the Millennium* that the physical heaven and Earth passed away and "a new heaven and a new earth" replaced them.

In 3050 AD, I live in a fully-restored universe. *The whole Universe* was restored to the pristine state of shimmering luminosity that it had before the Luciferian Fall (which preceded the Adamic Fall). My eternal somatic identity is substantive but its substantiality is not due to the material substance with which you are familiar. The physical elements with which you are familiar were *burned up,* or *consumed,* in the universal nuclear fission that occurred to all subatomic particles at the time of the creation of "a new heaven and a new earth" — as the Creator-God infused the physical universe with the spiritual supramolecules and divine Fire of His Sovereign and Supreme Being.

Although the final end-time Antichrist was overcome and destroyed at the beginning of *the Millennium,* mortality, corporeality, corporeal death, and *Hades* were not destroyed until the end of *the Millennium.* So, during *the Millennium,* corporeal beings were still required to work and toil by tilling the ground and fulfilling various other earthly responsibilities. Although the average human lifespan was drastically increased throughout *the Millennium,* human births and deaths still occurred during that period of time.

At the end of *the Millennium,* Satan, his fallen angels, and his unclean spirits were released from the holding tank where they had been imprisoned (i.e., *the bottomless pit of the Abyss in Hades).* Upon their release, they led a final rebellion against the Creator-God that included a significant number of human beings who lived on

Earth during *the Millennium*. The human beings who joined themselves to this final rebellion had become rebellious themselves, but, unlike rebellious human beings who had lived before *the Millennium,* they could not blame Satan and his evil forces for fueling or feeding their rebellious natures: They were rebellious: (1) because they refused to live their human lives in fealty to their Sovereign Lord, Christ Jesus; and (2) because they refused to live their human lives in self-discipline by abstaining from various lusts of the eye and flesh, including greed and immorality.

This final war occurred between: (1) Satan, his fallen angels, his unclean spirits, and rebellious human beings; and (2) the Lord Jesus Christ, his heavenly angels, his saints in Heaven, and his saints on Earth. You can think of this final war as *World War IV.* It differed from all other earlier world wars because each of the two warring factions included corporeal beings (i.e., human beings) as well as incorporeal beings (i.e., spiritual beings or discarnates). For the sake of clarity, the incorporeal beings included those who had once been human as well as those who had never been human (i.e., angels). Having been bought with the price of his shed blood at the cross on Calvary, I belonged to the Lord Jesus Christ. Therefore, during *World War IV,* I fought at his side along with all other created beings who also belonged to him. Because I had died before *the Millennium,* I fought as an incorporeal being.

This final battle, figuratively called the battle of *Gog and Magog* in Revelation 20:8, terminated all remaining powers of evil, including *Death* and everything associated with *Death:* (1) all iniquity, sin, sickness, disease, deterioration, disability, deformation, and physical death; (2) all corporeality; and (3) all realms and levels of mortal being in *Hell (Hades* or *Sheol).*

At the end of the final battle, Satan (an entity), *Death* (the corporeal condition, or incarnate mode of being, in mortality), and *Hell* (the incorporeal condition, or discarnate mode of being, in mortality) were thrown into *the Lake of Fire,* where (1) Mohammed and (2) the final end-time Antichrist had already been cast when Christ Jesus returned to Earth at the beginning of *the Millennium.* For the sake of clarification, *the Lake of Fire* is an eternal state and place of being that was created by the *Self-Existent One* (i.e., the one true and only real God and Creator of all that is) to mete out unending punishment to all who would consciously choose to be eternally disobedient to His Will. Just as the state of eternal redemption exists in eternity, so also does the state of eternal damnation exist in eternity. For the sake of clarity, *the Lake of Fire* is also known in the Holy Bible as *the second death.* (There is more about *Death, Hades,* and *the Lake of Fire* in Chapter Six and Appendix A of this book.)

The Great White Throne Judgment of God occurs at the end of *World War IV.* During that final judgment, all evil beings are immediately cast into *the Lake of Fire* and all remaining souls on Earth are appointed, according to their works while on Earth, either to eternal redemption in Heaven or eternal damnation in *the Lake of Fire.* Also at that time, all souls in *Hell (Hades* or *Sheol)* are judged according to their works. Finally, at the Great White Throne Judgment, all souls who had already been saved before *the Millennium* received specific rewards for their faithfulness to Christ Jesus during their sojourns in corporeality and for fulfilling the responsibilities God gave them to carry out during *the Millennium.* I saw all of this as it happened.

I not only watched what happened throughout *the Millennium,* I played an active role in carrying out the Will of the Creator-God — just as everyone else who belonged to Christ Jesus played an active role. At the end of *the Millennium* and after the Great White Throne Judgment, Christ Jesus presented his fully-restored creation to the Lord God Almighty (i.e., *God the Father),* who then infused the entire physical universe with the Totality of

His Being. The Totality of His Being included His Fiery Nature, which was mostly hidden from human beings during the seven thousand years of Biblical history in order to avoid expunging, or annihilating, them. This infusion caused the universal fission of physical elements that was mentioned previously. At the exact moment that the entire physical universe was infused with the Totality of the Creator-God's Sovereign and Supreme Being, the physical universe changed back to reflecting the Creator-God completely, wholly, and perfectly (i.e., it was returned to the state it was in before the Fall of Lucifer). It was at this moment that your current heaven and Earth *passed away*. (Again, "heaven" here represents the sky, the physical atmosphere, and the physical universe.) Now, in 3050 AD, the "new heaven" and "new earth" (Revelation 21:1) are completely different from that with which you are familiar. Finally, no part of *the whole Universe* remains altered because of iniquity and sin!

I know that those of you who study and understand Scripture (the Holy Bible is the only Scripture) would like a Scriptural reference to support what I have just presented. Here it is:

{24} [After the millennial reign of Christ Jesus] then comes the end, when he [God the Son] shall have delivered up the Kingdom to God, even the Father; when he [God the Son] shall have put down all rule and all authority and power. {25} For he [God the Son] must reign, until He [God the Father] has put all enemies under his [God the Son's] feet. {26} The last enemy that shall be destroyed is death [including mortality, corporeality, and physical death]. {27} For He [God the Father] has put all things under his [God the Son's] feet. But when he says all things are put under him [see Matthew 28:18 and John 5:26-27], it is manifest that an exception is He [God the Father] who put all things under him [God the Son]. {28} And when all things shall be subdued unto him [God the Son], then shall the Son also himself be subject unto Him [God the Father] that put all things under him [God the Son], that God [the Father] may be *All-in-all*.

1 Corinthians 15:24-28 KJV Paraphrase

In 1 Corinthians 15:24, *the Kingdom* refers to all that belongs to God the Son and has been placed under his feet (i.e., under his jurisdiction, authority, and power) by God the Father (see Matthew 28:18). That *the Kingdom is delivered up to God* means that it is *delivered up* to God the Father by God the Son. This event occurs after World War IV (i.e., the battle of Gog and Magog) and the Great White Throne Judgment (see Revelation 20:8 and 20:11-15 KJV). When God the Son *delivers up the Kingdom* to God the Father, God the Father completely infuses the physical universe with the Totality of His Being (i.e., the Glory of His Fiery Presence). The Glory of God the Father is then emitted as well as reflected throughout the entire universe by God the Son so that the two (God the Father and God the Son) are no longer distinguishable from one another and are no longer partitioned from one another — which partitioning was initiated by the Creator-God before the beginning of physical creation in order to implement His Plan of Salvation for the fallen Adamic Race of spiritual beings, who fell to the state of mortality after they were created. When *the Kingdom is delivered up,* what was One and became Three (i.e., God the Father, God the Son, and God the Holy Spirit) becomes One again. (God the Father, God the Son, and God the Holy Spirit are then fully recognized and understood by all created beings to be indivisibly one.) When *the Kingdom is delivered up* to God the Father by God the Son, all that has physical mass melts with "fervent heat" (2 Peter 3:10 KJV) — thereby releasing all subatomic energy it contains — and all released energy is then entirely reabsorbed by God the

Father. When *the Kingdom is delivered up,* there is an involution of temporality into eternity. In other words, temporality and corporeality are "swallowed up" in victory by the Creator-God's eternal Life (1 Corinthians 15:54 KJV and 2 Corinthians 5:4 KJV).

Even though I had received a new somatic identity at the time when Christ Jesus returned to Earth, my somatic identity received a refreshing at the time that the Creator-God infused the entire physical universe with the Totality of His Being (i.e., the instant that the Creator-God became "All-in-all"). Just like all other restored created beings, I became eternally infused by the spiritual supramolecules and divine Fire of the Creator-God's Sovereign and Supreme Being that admixed with the spiritual molecules of my own relatively-new somatic identity (which, by then, was only one thousand years old according to your measure of time). This infusion formed the glowing, pulsating body that I now have and will always have throughout all eternity. The Supraconsciousness of the Creator-God was also forever co-mingled with my own individual consciousness. Like all of my spiritual siblings saved by the shed blood of Christ Jesus, I now have spiritual light burning within me from the eternal flame of the Creator-God's Holy Spirit, and I now have an outer spiritual glow from the heavenly Glory of God reflected by the supernatural molecules of my own *astral gelatinous*™ somatic identity. In these ways, all residents in eternity are *enlightened* like the burning bush encountered by Moses: Although we are burning, we are not *burned up* (i.e., we are neither melted nor consumed).

There is substance in eternity but not the substance with which you are familiar. Spiritual substance is different from physical substance (i.e., ordinary matter), just as spiritual flesh (i.e., *astral gelatinous*™ flesh) is different from physical flesh (i.e., *protoplasmic* flesh). Both spiritual substance and physical substance are substantive but only to the people who live in their respective states and loci of being. All beings in eternity see physical substance as translucent but see spiritual substance as tangible. Conversely, all beings in temporality see spiritual substance as translucent (when they are exposed to it) but see physical substance as tangible.

Perhaps the greatest fear in being human is the fear of losing one's identity and volitional self-awareness at the time of one's physical death (hence the fear of death itself). Human beings are afraid of having their lives extinguished. However, although that fear is understandable, that fear is unfounded because all saved souls retain their individual identities and volitional self-awareness in God throughout all eternity. *For example,* in eternity I have retained an individual identity at the same time that I have a compound, composite, and corporate identity in Christ Jesus. Do not misconclude that I have multiple identities: I have only one identity and that identity is spiritually concorporeal with all other individuals who live, move, and have their being in Christ Jesus. I have not lost my *self* (i.e., my individual personality, free will, and self-awareness). Rather, I have regained my *Self* (i.e., my personal identity in the Creator-God through the shed blood of Christ Jesus). I have never felt as alive as I do now. I have never felt as actualized as I do now. I have never felt as relevant and cherished as I do now. It eventually dawns on all of us who are destined for eternity that we were never created to constitute a whole as individual beings; instead, we were created to be parts of a unified whole that only exists in and through Christ Jesus, who is the spoken Word, or divine Logos, of the Creator-God. My membership in this unified whole has imparted an indescribable feeling of satisfaction, peace, and connectedness to me that never leaves me. I work cooperatively, never competitively, with all other created beings in eternity who are either (1) unfallen or (2) completely restored as if they had never been fallen.

At the time of the Creator-God's infusion of the Totality of His Being into the entire physical universe, my individual consciousness was co-mingled with the Supraconsciousness of the Creator-God. So, although I am not the Creator-God, and never will become the Creator-God, I am now interfaced by Him and fused to Him. The supernatural molecules of my being are eternally admixed with the spiritual supramolecules and divine Fire of His Sovereign and Supreme Being. Because of this, my knowledge and understanding have been multiplied exponentially and explosively. I now understand what I never could have understood while I was a human being. My referent is completely and permanently changed.

Earlier in this chapter, I stated that your chronological time is curvilinear but not circular. Think of your chronological time as a major thoroughfare that permits traffic flow in one direction, and one direction only, with various sets of entrance ramps and exit ramps for each individual soul. A major entrance ramp that you use corresponds with your transition into the earth plane of consciousness at the specific time that your soul enters physicality while your human body is developing within your mother's uterus. A major exit ramp that you use corresponds with your transition from the earth plane of consciousness to the next plane of consciousness that you are destined to enter. Except for people: (1) who have *near death experiences* (NDEs), (2) who experience *astral projection,* or (3) who have multiple human lives, there is only one major entrance ramp and one major exit ramp for each person.

To be sure, during your lifetime, you cannot time travel at will on that thoroughfare (i.e., jump from one period of chronological time to another period of chronological time). However, exceptions do occur based on the Will of the Creator-God. Exceptions include: (1) people who have *near death experiences* that momentarily *pop into* eternity and are permitted or required (depending on the person, the person's needs, and the Will of the Creator-God) to regain entrance to their original segment of curvilinear chronological time after their short sojourn in eternity; (2) people who experience astral projection that momentarily *pop into* eternity and *pop back* to their original segment of curvilinear chronological time exactly where they left off; and (3) people who actually leave temporality (i.e., relative space-time) for an extended period of chronological time only to reenter the thoroughfare of curvilinear chronological time in a later segment to re-experience corporeality in an additional human lifetime.

In summary, because of the constraints imposed on them by curvilinear chronological time, the souls of human beings are not able to *time travel* unless: (1) they have a *near death experience;* (2) they project astrally during an altered state of consciousness (like the Apostle John did when he saw the future that he recorded in the Book of Revelation); or (3) they are permitted by the Creator-God to *pop into* an incorporeal realm only to reemerge somewhere else on the thoroughfare of curvilinear chronological time in an additional human life (to be sure, there is a locus of incorporeality for those who are in between human lives).

All three types of time travel experiences presented in the previous paragraph are only initiated by the Creator-God and never initiated by the individuals who have the experiences. Permission is granted by the Creator-God to time travel only if it fits into His Will concerning His design for us all individually, collectively, and corporately. *For example,* the Creator-God might want the time traveler to learn what happened in the past or what will happen in the future in order to report back to others to help clarify for them: (1) what happened and why it happened; or (2) what will happen and why it will happen. In the case of the latter, the Creator-God might want the time traveler to learn what will occur in the future in order to report back to others in order to help an individual, or an entire social group, prepare for or avoid one specific outcome or a set of outcomes — like the Prophet Jonah did for the people of Nineveh (i.e., an ancient city adjacent to the current city of Mosul in Iraq). In either of these two cases, the time traveler is an observer only and cannot alter events or outcomes while the events and outcomes are being observed. Finally, the Lord God Almighty might want a soul to learn additional lessons, or demonstrate and share what it has learned from its past lessons, by experiencing human life again. (If you have not yet read Appendix A and Appendix B, now would be a good time for you to do that.)

Chapter Two

The Role of Human Flesh during *the Millennium*

Human flesh has always had a mind of its own. And that mind is called *carnal mind* in the King James Version of the Holy Bible. Throughout all of the millennia since the Adamic Fall until the creation of "a new heaven and a new earth" (Revelation 21:1 KJV), human flesh, and the carnal mind that directs it, were always opposed to the Will and Spirit of God. Human flesh, and the carnal mind that directs it, always played a prominent role in the disobedience of human beings to the Will and Spirit of God during that time — from the Adamic Fall (but not as a cause for the Adamic Fall) to the creation of "a new heaven and a new earth" — due to the yielding of human beings to the temptations of their own flesh (James 1:14-15). However, human flesh, and the carnal mind that directs it, jointly played their greatest seditious role, proportionately so, during the millennium of peace (i.e., *the Millennium*) that Christ Jesus reigned on Earth. Why? During *the Millennium,* Satan and his evil forces, including his fallen angels and unclean spirits (the latter of which are the discarnate souls of the evil dead), were no longer able to influence human beings by: (1) inflaming their lusts, (2) implanting images in their susceptible minds, or (3) inhabiting their souls (and, in turn, possessing their human bodies). At the end of *the Tribulation,* when Christ Jesus returned to Earth, Satan and his evil forces were altogether incapacitated because the director of their collective consciousness (i.e., Satan) and his minions were imprisoned. Thus, in addition to the activity of Satan, the activity of all fallen angels and unclean spirits also ceased during *the Millennium:* The evil motives of all evil forces were frozen, so to speak, by their spiritual inaccessibility to human beings.

As a side note here, Good (i.e., Righteousness) and Evil (i.e., Unrighteousness) each have a collective consciousness based on their motives. The motive for all righteous beings is to please the Lord God Almighty. The motive for all unrighteous beings is to conquer the Lord God Almighty and His righteous beings by dividing them all from one another.

To reiterate as well as to further dissect my explanation for the purpose of reinforcing a greater understanding, throughout *the Millennium* — which is to say, the 1,000 years of peace during which Christ Jesus reigned on Earth — there was no external evil activity on Earth. External evil activity did not resume until the end of *the Millennium,* which end culminated in World War IV — referred to as the Battle of Gog and Magog in Revelation 20:8. There was no external evil activity throughout *the Millennium* for these two primary reasons: *First,* Christ Jesus was reigning on Earth, and the reign of Christ Jesus on Earth itself suppressed external evil activity because of the ubiquitous presence of God's Holy Spirit that had been poured out on all humankind (Joel 2:28; Acts 2:17). *Second,* Satan and his followers had been bound, or imprisoned, in the "bottomless pit" for the entire 1,000 years of *the Millennium* (Revelation 20:2-3; Isaiah 21-22): That they had been bound not only incapacitated Satan's evil influence on human beings but also the evil influence on human beings by all of his hordes. However, although humanity did not have to fight against Satan's mortal mind (the collective consciousness of Evil), humanity did have to fight daily throughout *the Millennium* against its own flesh and the carnal mind that directs it.

During *the Millennium,* human beings could not claim, or even think to claim, that Satan's mortal mind led them to commit sinful acts. All wrongful acts committed by human beings during *the Millennium* were entirely of their own choosing and doing. Thus, there was an even greater responsibility, proportionately so, placed on human beings during *the Millennium* to override the desires of their own flesh, and the carnal mind that directs those desires, by "bringing into captivity every thought to the obedience of Christ" (2 Corinthians 10:5 KJV). Why? The desires of carnal mind are incapable of reining themselves in.

During *the Millennium,* human beings were still subjected to their own fears, lusts, selfishness, pretentiousness, ignorance, malice, and covetousness. During *the Millennium,* human beings still entertained unclean thoughts, feelings, ideas, associations, images, and affiliations — specifically those of a sexual, earthy, worldly, egotistical, cunning, conniving, selfish, fearful, carnal, narcissistic, arrogant, condemning, judgmental, irreverent, vulgar, willful, wasteful, lustful, unforgiving, resentful, impatient, thieving, addicting, haughty, prejudicial, vengeful, and immature nature. During *the Millennium,* the only difference was that Satan and his evil forces and their collective consciousness (i.e., *Satan's mortal mind)* were no longer able to spark, ignite, inflame, or fan those unclean thoughts, feelings, ideas, associations, images, and affiliations: During *the Millennium,* people on Earth did that entirely on their own without the aid of any unseen evil force. It was in this way that there was a greater burden, proportionately so, placed on one's control over his or her own flesh, and the carnal mind that directs it, during *the Millennium.*

Here are some practical recommendations for people to remember during *the Millennium*. Throughout *the Millennium,* human beings should be ever vigilant:

> Because the carnal mind [i.e., the mind operating according to fleshly desires] is enmity against God [i.e., in direct opposition to God], it is not subject to the law of God — neither, indeed, can it be.
>
> *Romans 8:6-7 KJV Paraphrase*

> Human beings must always watch and pray that they do not enter into temptation; although God's Holy Spirit in one's soul is ever willing to do the right thing, human flesh is ever weak to do the wrong thing.
>
> *Matthew 26:41 KJV Paraphrase*

> It is God's Holy Spirit that makes alive; human flesh, and the carnal mind that directs it, profit nothing.
>
> *John 6:63a KJV Paraphrase*

> If human beings live after the flesh, then they will die. But if they live through God's Holy Spirit, they mortify the deeds of the human body, and they will remain alive.
>
> *Romans 8:13 KJV Paraphrase*

> Those who belong to Christ Jesus crucify [i.e., in daily self-sacrifice] the human body with its lusts and desires.
>
> *Galatians 5:24 KJV Paraphrase*

Because there will continue to be a tendency for human beings to rationalize and justify sin during *the Millennium,* a solid understanding of abnormal psychology, psychoanalysis, and psychotherapy will be useful during that period of time for faith practitioners to knowledgeably inform themselves and others: (1)

why human beings do the things they do; (2) how to overcome what they do that is harmful to themselves, to each other, and to their relationships; and (3) how to override as well as undo what they have a tendency to do because they are still in the flesh. However, studying and applying psychological principles does not mean that, during *the Millennium,* human beings should abandon studying and applying principles of *Christ consciousness, the Supra-consciousness of God,* or *divine Mind* (all three italicized phrases are used synonymously here) in favor of behaviorism, family systems theory and therapy, or any other psychoanalytical systems, methodologies, or tools.

Although God's Holy Spirit is freely poured out on all flesh throughout *the Millennium,* sins of the flesh are still attractive to souls that remain in a corporeal condition. That is why there is still a tendency during *the Millennium* to hide personal sin, especially through self-rationalization and self-justification. Just because the Lord Jesus is on Earth during *the Millennium,* or just because God's Holy Spirit daily falls afresh on the people of God throughout *the Millennium,* does not mean that the entire Earth turns into some giant cultish commune with the exchanging of flowers and peace signs or other gratuitous, superficial expressions of love.

Author's Note: There are additional reasons that abnormal psychology, psychoanalysis, and psychotherapy remain useful to faith practitioners during *the Millennium. For example,* human beings will still possess their so-called "rat" and "reptilian" brain centers (formally referred to as the mesolimbic pathway and brain stem), which are brain areas responsible for: (1) involuntary reflexes that control thoughts, emotions, and behaviors related to seeking comfort, avoiding discomfort, and surviving instinctively as well as (2) learned disordered thoughts, emotions, and behaviors related to addiction, compulsion, and inferior education, training, and nurturance. Moreover, during *the Millennium,* human beings will still be subjected to: (1) their own inherited, idiosyncratic personalities, dispositions, and temperaments; (2) their own animal instincts — including brutality, sexual lust, jealousy, and envy; and (3) tragic and traumatic accidents and severe physical, mental, and emotional injuries that happen to themselves and their loved ones. During *the Millennium,* human beings will even continue to experience flesh-related insecurities.

To be sure, human flesh is a formidable foe to living according to the Will and Spirit of God. The carnal mind that directs human flesh forever stands opposed to God's Holy Spirit and Will. The Spirit of God within men and women always stands ready to overcome, but the flesh is always prone to fail because it is weak, frail, and erring (Matthew 26:41). That is why, during *the Millennium,* human beings will continue to deal with inner conflicts and imbalances physically and psychologically as well as metaphysically, spiritually, and supernaturally in order to have daily victory over their ongoing personality predispositions, animal instincts, and traumatic experiences.

During *the Millennium,* human flesh, and the carnal mind that directs it, prove that not all intrusive thoughts and emotions originate from Satan, his fallen angels, or his unclean spirits. During *the Millennium,* the origin of unclean thoughts and feelings is from one's own flesh and the carnal mind that directs it.

Roundabout Number Three

Conflicts that have their Origin in Flesh

1. Taxes

Taxes (pronounced *taks'-eez*) are responses to external stimuli by animals. (Tropisms are responses to external stimuli by plants.) Common examples of taxes include barotaxes, chemotaxes, hydrotaxes, phototaxes, and thermotaxes. A taxis (singular of *taxes*) is considered: (1) a positive taxis if an organism moves or reorients itself *toward* the applied environmental stimulus or (2) a negative taxis if an organism moves or reorients itself *away from* the applied environmental stimulus. Responses to taxes are considered innate behaviors because they are fixed and unchanging for a species. *Examples* of taxes for the human body include most nonspecific defense mechanisms as well as some specific defense mechanisms related to immunity.

Other innate behaviors for the human body include physiologically-induced and physiologically-mediated responses such as: (1) uncontrolled and unlearned reflexes, (2) instincts, (3) hyperarousal, (4) clitoral and penile engorgement with blood, and (5) libido-related *presenting* and *mounting* (which are more obvious in primates other than human beings).

Innate behaviors are introduced in this roundabout to help readers understand that, during *the Millennium,* human beings will continue to wrestle with their own flesh and the carnal mind that directs it.

2. Physiologically-Based Inner Conflicts

Neurohormones and Neuromodulators

The nervous system and the endocrine system regulate and coordinate various innate activities of the human body. In many cases, the nervous and endocrine systems overlap in regulating and coordinating physiologic processes. *For example,* some substances are produced that function as both hormones and neurotransmitters. (Such substances are often referred to as "neurohormones.") In general, neurohormones belong either to the category of *biogenic amines* or the category of *neuropeptides.* Examples of prominent biogenic amines that function as neurohormones include epinephrine (adrenaline) and norepinephrine (noradrenaline). Both epinephrine and norepinephrine are synthesized in the adrenal medulla (which is derived from embryonic neural tissue); norepinephrine is also synthesized in: (1) the loci cerulei (singular *locus ceruleus*) of the pons in the brain stem (*ceruleus* is also spelled *coeruleus*) and (2) the sympathetic nervous system. Epinephrine and norepinephrine are included in this roundabout because they are examples of substances that will continue during *the Millennium* to contribute to physiologically-induced and physiologically-mediated inner conflicts that are innate to human behavior and influence well-being.

Sex steroid hormones — including progesterone as well as various estrogens and androgens — are not considered neurotransmitters or neurohormones. However, sex steroid hormones can be thought of as neuromodulators because of their major feedback and regulatory impacts on brain physiology that influence mood, affect (i.e., observable manifestations of emotion), arousal, satiety, pleasure, anxiety, depression, rage, aggression, libido, and specific behaviors related to sexual affinity. Sex steroid hormones are also included in this roundabout because they are examples of substances that will continue during *the Millennium* to contribute to physiologically-induced and physiologically-mediated inner conflicts that are innate to human behavior and influence well-being.

The actions of epinephrine, norepinephrine, and sex steroid hormones help students of the Holy Bible understand that human beings have always wrestled with their own flesh and blood (i.e., their own physiologically-induced and physiologically-mediated inner conflicts) in addition to whatever spiritual enemies with which they have also wrestled.

The Holy Bible is clear that, from the time of the Adamic Fall until the beginning of *the Millennium,* the most significant battlefield for human beings was in the spiritual realm:

> For we wrestle not against flesh and blood, but against principalities, against powers, against the rulers of the darkness of this world, and against spiritual wickedness in high places.
>
> *Ephesians 4:12 KJV*

The passage of Scripture just quoted refers to external evil forces and power struggles *before* the return of Christ Jesus to Earth for *the Millennium,* but the passage does not refer to inner conflicts induced or mediated by neurohormones or neuromodulators. Indeed, human beings have always regularly fought the effects of neurohormones and neuromodulators that: (1) heighten fear, rage, and aggression; (2) stimulate the libido as well as various associated sexual behaviors; and (3) heighten abilities during predatory activities (either when one is stalking or when one is being stalked). Abilities heightened during predatory activities include arousal (i.e., hyperarousal), vigilance (i.e., hypervigilance), and strategizing (i.e., using cunning logistics) — all of which translate to a jungle or forest environment just as well as they translate to a school or office environment (in subtler ways, of course, in the case of a school or office environment).

All human beings during *the Millennium* will continue to wrestle with the urges of their own individual flesh and the carnal mind that directs it. They will continue to wrestle with their own behaviors, attitudes, and activities that stem from the production of certain neurohormones and neuromodulators. In other words, they will continue to wrestle with positive and negative feedback mechanisms that stimulate behaviors, attitudes, and activities that seem to be uncontrollable and, in some cases, *are* uncontrollable. They will continue to wrestle with various addictions, including those promoted by the biochemical rushes induced from spectator sports, daredevil activities, sexual orgasms, predatory behaviors, and general risk-taking *(for example,* in participatory sports, illicit activities, and legal gambling). What plagued human beings who lived before *the Millennium* will also plague human beings who live during *the Millennium*. To be sure, human conflicts during *the Millennium* are not with external evil forces; they are with individual physiological responses as well as with group biology. In these ways, human beings have wrestled with their own flesh and the carnal mind that directs it, and they will continue to wrestle with them during *the Millennium*.

Although human beings continue during *the Millennium* to wrestle with their own flesh and the carnal mind that directs it, they can still turn to God for spiritual, emotional, mental, and physical help in combating, refocusing, and overturning their own animal instincts and biologically-driven predispositions. To be sure, such victories are never easy. One can sense the Apostle Paul's frustration with his own flesh and blood in his statement:

"I do not do the good that I want to do, but I do the evil that I do not want to do" (Romans 7:19 KJV Paraphrase), which precipitated this following conclusion with its accompanying question:

O wretched man that I am! Who will deliver me from this [fleshly] body of death?
Romans 7:24 KJV Paraphrase

The Apostle Paul knew that the only way for human beings to overcome physiologically-induced and physiologically-mediated temptations is by crucifying, or sacrificing, their own flesh:

Knowing this, that when our carnal man is crucified with Christ Jesus, the body of sin [i.e., the power of human flesh to tempt] is destroyed in order that we should not serve sin.
Romans 6:6 KJV Paraphrase

It is difficult for many people to accept that their souls live in the bodies of human animals. They refuse to acknowledge that human beings are part of the Animal Kingdom. They would rather not concede that human beings are vertebrates, mammals, and primates. For them, the dichotomy between the spiritual and natural is contrived or insulting to God as well as to humankind. They don't want to know that individual physiology and group biology shape instincts, habits, personality, gender identity, and sexual orientation. They don't want to know that conditions like Tourette syndrome, schizophrenia, and criminal insanity are of biochemical, and not demonic, origin.

Dietary Intake, Fasting, and Microbiota

The interplay of an individual's hunger and satiety in connection to his/her dietary intake is also relevant to a discussion of physiologically-induced and physiologically-mediated inner conflicts that are innate to human behavior and influence well-being during *the Millennium.*

For example, the effect of ingesting too much refined sugar, in combination with the body's own natural insulin production in response to such ingestion (assuming normalcy of cellular insulin receptor number, structure, and function), triggers an addictive pleasurable rush that can lead to long term compulsive overeating and obesity.

During *the Millennium,* fasting will still play a role in *ecstasis* and the revelation of intellectual and spiritual truth (see Author's Note in the next paragraph for the definition of *ecstasis).* Planned intermittent fasting and prolonged fasting can result in beneficial fasting ketosis (not to be confused with diabetic ketoacidosis from decreased insulin activity), which contributes to enhanced mental clarity plus heightened sensitivity and receptivity to the thoughts and feelings of others (including those from corporeal and incorporeal life forms as well as those from the Supraconsciousness of the Creator-God Himself).

Author's Note: *Ecstasis* comes from the Greek word ἔκστασις (ek´-sta-sis) [G1611] that refers to a trance-like state induced by the Holy Spirit. This Greek word is specifically translated as "trance" in the King James Version of the Holy Bible, denoting the state into which both the Apostle Peter and the Apostle Paul fell (Acts 10:10; 11:5; 22:17) when they each had visions induced by the Creator-God's Holy Spirit as they were praying.

During *the Millennium,* another example of physiologically-induced and physiologically-mediated inner conflicts that are innate to human behavior and influence well-being comes from bacterial colonies in the gut.

Without an included definition, the word *gut* is an imprecise word. Here, the present author means *gut* to include the stomach, small intestine, and large intestine (i.e., the gastrointestinal tract). Bacteria in the gut are part of each human being's *microbiome* or *microbiota* along with protists, archaea, viruses, and fungi. Normally, the relationship of gut microbiota to human beings is not merely commensal (a non-harmful coexistence) but mutualistic (reciprocally beneficial). Of course, overgrowth of normally-beneficial bacteria and growth of harmful bacteria can contribute to illnesses related not only to malabsorption but also absorption of toxins in the gut. Dilemmas associated with microbiota in the gut, especially in relationship to overeating and eating insensibly, will continue for human beings throughout *the Millennium.*

Victorious Living

During *the Millennium,* human beings must think (1) spiritually (that is, prayerfully and metaphysically) and (2) intelligently (that is, rationally and logically) if they are to have victory over animal instincts and biologically-driven predispositions and influences. Following are five examples of flesh and blood conflicts over which human beings can have victory during *the Millennium* through understanding God's absolute truth:

First, epinephrine (adrenaline), produced by the adrenal medulla, is responsible for physiologic responses to stress caused by perceived threats from environmental stimuli. Produced in response to perceived threats, epinephrine enables human beings to have enough energy, oxygen, and blood flow: (1) to stay and defend themselves or (2) to turn and flee. That is why epinephrine is partly responsible for the *fight-or-flight response*. However, spiritually-minded people know that there is a third option other than fleeing or fighting: (3) They can remain exactly where they are — not to fight but to love and forgive and trust in God. In other words, they can muster the necessary courage to transcend and override their individual physiology and biochemistry. This broadens possible responses from just *fight-or-flight* to *fight-or-flight-or-freeze*. Human beings can have the presence of mind in Christ Jesus to stand by faith (i.e., *freeze*) without yielding to their fear and epinephrine's physiologic imperatives for physical actions and reactions.

Second, sometimes the combined effects of epinephrine and the brain's enkephalins, endorphins, and dynorphins (i.e., the brain's so-called *natural opioids*) trigger an addictive pleasurable "rush" from extreme sports, daredevil activities, and other forms of risk-taking like gambling and participating in illicit activities. However, through Christ Jesus, spiritually-minded individuals can transcend and override their desires to experience this rush by refusing in Christ Jesus to put themselves in potentially harmful, dangerous, and unhealthy situations that are addictive in nature, tempting, and unwise.

Third, scientific research has demonstrated the inordinate amount of time that human beings — especially males during their sexual prime — devote to thinking about sexual intercourse in their own related imagery due to high concentrations of androgens. Although some males may use these biological predispositions to justify their having sex with as many partners as possible or having extramarital affairs, such behaviors do not live up to God's ideal of faithfulness to one covenant-based, lifelong spousal partner. However, through Christ Jesus, human beings living during *the Millennium* will be able to continue to transcend and override the unhealthy and immoral urges of mammalian group biology *(unhealthy* and *immoral* for human beings but not for other mammals).

Fourth, through Christ Jesus, spiritually-minded individuals living during *the Millennium* can transcend and override their desires to re-experience a sugar-induced rush by regularly fasting and, as a result, not only achieve a healthier body but also heighten their sensitivity and receptivity to spiritual communications.

Fifth, to help avoid various harmful gut-related syndromes, individuals living during *the Millennium* need to be thoroughly schooled in how to maintain homeostasis in their bodies through understanding proper nutrition and dietary intake. Therefore, all medical practitioners and faith practitioners living during *the Millennium* need to teach: (1) how to maintain a steady state of equilibrium in one's body through proper nutrition and dietary intake, (2) the favorable effects of intermittent and prolonged fasting on the central nervous system (CNS) and spiritual communications (expressive as well as receptive forms), and (3) the influences of metabolites from intestinal bacterial colonies on one's physical, mental, and emotional well-being.

Summary

If you believe that, during *the Millennium,* not one human being will: (1) be involved in a fist fight, (2) masturbate, (3) participate in dangerous activities, (4) be killed in an accident, (5) overeat or eat insensibly, (6) become ill from microbiotic imbalances within the gut, or (7) commit a sin, please be advised that you are wrong. All human beings living during *the Millennium* will still have their own human flesh to contend with.

Hormones, neurotransmitters, neurohormones, neuromodulators, diet, and microbial life forms can often make human beings victims of their own animal natures, biological predispositions, and/or unhealthy decisions. The only way that human beings can become victors over their own physiology is for them to understand who they are as animals at the same time that they understand who they are as spiritual beings in Christ Jesus. Refocusing their attention away from biological imperatives and thoughts associated with addictive, immoral, and unhealthy behaviors to absolute spiritual truth by: (1) meditating on God's written Word, (2) fasting, and (3) praying to God is still requisite during *the Millennium* if human beings are to overcome temptations from their own flesh, the carnal mind that directs it, and environmental factors they may not be able to control.

End of Roundabout Number Three

Chapter Three

Governance on Earth during *the Millennium*

The Human Population remaining on Earth after the Tribulation

During *the Tribulation* (the seven-year period of time that preceded the return of Christ Jesus to Earth), the human population of Earth had been apocalyptically reduced by: (1) plagues, including increased mortality from coronavirus and pox variants and mutations; (2) pestilences, including worldwide deforestation and devegetation through the explosive growth of denitrifying bacteria; (3) wars, including the mutually-assured destruction of nations from nuclear bombs and their radiation; (4) famines, including substantially decreased agricultural production from heightened solar activity, detrimental soil and climate changes, drought, and polluted waters; (5) urban crime, including an increase in murder from rampant lawlessness and anarchy; (6) harmful climate changes, including elevated temperatures from greenhouse gas emission, volcanic ash production, and a depleted ozone layer; (7) harmful geologic changes, including increased earthquakes from massive tectonic plate upheavals and rising sea levels from melting polar ice caps; (8) impoverished economic conditions, including the collapse of all national currencies and banking systems; (9) the instantaneous removal of wicked people from Earth by angels of the Creator-God, including their harvest by reaper-angels before Christ Jesus set foot on Earth (see Matthew 13:24-30, 36-43; Acts 1:9-11);

and (10) the instantaneous removal of pre-millennial Christians by their rapture (bodily resurrection) at the appearance of Christ Jesus on Earth's horizon.

During *the Millennium,* the substantially-reduced human population remaining on Earth consisted of Gentiles and Jews/Israelites who had been reconciled to Christ Jesus upon his appearing and who then became known as *Gentile Christians* or *Israelite Christians,* depending on heritage. Before *the Tribulation,* there had been a population on Earth of approximately 7.6 billion Gentiles and 14.7 million Jews/Israelites. At the end of *the Tribulation,* only 760 million Gentiles and 1.4 million Jews/Israelites remained.

The Necessity for Governance during the Millennium

During *the Millennium,* the governance of all people remaining on Earth was necessary because souls who lived on Earth were still in human flesh bodies. In other words, they still possessed protoplasmic somatic identities that predisposed them toward sinfulness. Thus, the will of human flesh continued to be a problem for obeying the Will of the Creator-God because the will of human flesh is irrevocably contrary to the Will of the Creator-God. The Prophet Isaiah understood just how contrary the nature of human flesh is to the nature of the Creator-God when he declared: "In seeing God, I will be annihilated because I am a person of iniquity" (Isaiah 6:5 KJV Paraphrase) – meaning, "I still possess human flesh, and human flesh cannot exist in the presence of God." Jude went so far as to state that human beings should even "hate the garment spotted, stained, or soiled by human flesh" (Jude 1:23 Paraphrase). Remember, human flesh is the outward sign of iniquity imposed as a curse by the Creator-God on errant souls who turned eons ago from obeying Him.

By virtue of their residing in human flesh, all human beings are naturally double-minded. For this reason, it is the daily responsibility of each individual to override his or her fleshly desires. This kind of double-mindedness never stops; it continues for the duration of one's human existence. However, the power that this double-mindedness has over human beings can diminish by praying, meditating on God's written word in the Holy Bible, refocusing one's attention, and obeying basic rules for righteous living. Employing these four activities during *the Millennium* helped righteous souls in human bodies avoid jumping the tracks on which they were travelling (and wanted to remain travelling).

One source, if not the greatest source, of frustration had always existed in the expectation that one's own double-mindedness would cease while one was still in human flesh. Thinking that the unholy and ungodly thoughts and feelings of their human flesh could be permanently extinguished while they were still on Earth had always been an unreasonable expectation and the source of much unnecessary guilt, shame, and self-castigation for human beings who desired to please the Creator-God. Because it was easily confused, the human brain misconcluded that there existed just one river of consciousness for each human being to channel; however, there were two different rivers of consciousness flowing at that time. One river was pure and untainted, and the other river was poisonous and polluted. Which river of thought that one was channeling and streaming is what determined the purity or impurity of one's thinking and feeling and, therefore, one's actions.

During *the Millennium* — (1) although all wicked people had been removed from Earth, and (2) although Christ Jesus was ruling on Earth from Jerusalem, and (3) although the Creator-God's Holy Spirit was continually poured out on all human inhabitants of Earth, and (4) although all demonic forces were restricted from influencing and inhabiting souls in human flesh — individuals, families, and communities of the remaining human population still had to contend with ungodly pulls from their own human flesh and the carnal mind that directs it, which pulls were forever in contention with the Will of the Creator-God.

Through the outpouring of the Creator-God's Holy Spirit, people living on Earth during *the Millennium* were able to recognize Good from Evil, but they still needed to have laws, rules, regulations, and ordinances (1) to help teach them right from wrong as well as (2) to habituate reasonable behaviors expected of them by their Creator and fellow citizens. For these purposes, formal governance was required for all human beings living during *the Millennium.*

The Hierarchic Structure of Governance during the Millennium

During *the Millennium,* God the Father remained resident in what the present author refers to in his writings as the spiritually-observable universe, which he uses synonymously with *Heaven* and *Eternity. Heaven* is the *state of being* and *Eternity* is the *place of being* in the spiritually-observable universe. Absolute space is *Heaven* and absolute time is *Eternity.* In *Heaven,* time is not a sequence of related events as it is in the physically-observable universe. In *Heaven,* time is actually *place.* Remember, space and time are fused and congruent in the spiritually-observable universe. There, God the Father remained poised to infuse the physically-observable universe with the totality of His Fiery Being at the end of *the Millennium.* For the sake of clarification, the spiritually-observable universe is also the state and place where souls saved before *the Millennium* co-mingled, and still co-mingle, with the Essence of Deity.

Regardless of God the Father's eternal residence in the spiritually-observable universe, His luminous Presence regularly inhabited the Inner Sanctuary, or Most Holy Place (i.e., the Holy of Holies), in the Millennial Jerusalem Temple (Beit HaMikdash in Yehovahsham, the new name for Jerusalem during the Millennium).

Before *the Millennium,* God the Father delegated to God the Son all power in the physically-observable universe — which, of course, includes heaven and Earth *(heaven* used here in the sense of the Earth's atmosphere and all outer space and its contents). During *the Millennium,* God the Son was resident in the physically-observable universe as the omnipotent, omnipresent, and omniscient power of Deity in corporeality. In corporeality, God the Son transcended relative space-time and could appear in multiple physical places at once, where he materialized, dematerialized, and rematerialized at will in his *astral gelatinous*™, *metacrystalline, supraplasmic,* or *glorified* body (the italicized qualifiers used here are discussed in Roundabout Number Two of Chapter One). Although resident in the physically-observable universe, God the Son also had complete access to the entire spiritually-observable universe.

Before *the Millennium,* all souls of *the first resurrection,* who had received their new somatic identities at the time of the Rapture, also existed (like God the Son) in *astral gelatinous*™, *metacrystalline, supraplasmic,* or *glorified* bodies and were able to materialize, dematerialize, and rematerialize on Earth at will. Our intermittent presence on Earth was important to governance as spiritual advisors, educators, and special representatives of Deity. Collectively, we had been delegated by Christ Jesus to advise both Gentile Christians and Israelite Christians during *the Millennium.*

Among Israelite Christians, a Sanhedrin Council of Seven was established as a governing body for their nation. Members of the Sanhedrin were drawn from the highest-ranking priests of

Righteousness (i.e., the sons of Zadok), who not only ministered to God the Father within the Inner Sanctuary but also served as judges in Israel. Among Gentile Christians, a Council of Seventy was established as a collective governing body for their nations. Local councils of elders and hosts for collective worship also existed in every nation. Fivefold Christian ministries of apostles, prophets, evangelists, pastors, and teachers no longer existed for Gentile Christians because that particular hierarchy was no longer necessary.

Governance of Israelite Christians during the Millennium

Pre-millennial Christians never supplanted, superseded, or replaced the nation of Israel literally, figuratively, or metaphysically as the chosen people of the Creator-God. Rather, pre-millennial Christians were simply *added* to the chosen people of the Creator-God — just as Gentile Christians and Israelite Christians belonged to the same Body of Christ during *the Millennium.*

Israelite Christians during *the Millennium* had specific roles to play overseeing activities in the Millennial Jerusalem Temple (Beit HaMikdash in Yehovahsham) as well as in celebrating various Feasts/Festivals of Worship and Remembrance in Jerusalem and throughout Israel.

Throughout *the Millennium,* 144,000 Israelite Christians ministered to the Lord God Almighty in Jerusalem (twelve thousand designated from each of the twelve tribes of Israel). Although the original 144,000 were first ordained and consecrated ("sealed") for specific service to the Lord God Almighty during *the Tribulation* (Revelation 7:4; 14:1 & 3), their tribal representation in the same numbers continued throughout *the Millennium.* Their service not only included specific responsibilities for worship in the magnificent and breathtakingly-beautiful Millennial Jerusalem

Temple but also for general governance in Israel. One group of these ministering Israelite Christians was consecrated in service to offer temple sacrifices to the Lord God Almighty as acts of atonement, worship, commemoration, and sanctification. Sacrificial atonement was practiced specifically for these three reasons: (1) reconciliation for the nation of Israel; (2) transgressions committed during the Millennium, and (3) purification of human iniquity still present because of the continued existence of souls in corporeality (i.e., in forms of human flesh).

Governance of Gentile Christians during the Millennium

Although Good and Evil were recognizable to all people living on Earth during *the Millennium,* the precepts of the Creator-God needed to be written on their hearts and minds. How could precepts be written on the hearts and minds of men and women if the precepts had not already been codified?

Where did Gentile Christians look for the laws that would be written on their hearts and minds? They did not turn to the more than 600 rules, regulations, and ordinances found in Torah (also known as the *Pentateuch* or first five books of the Bible), which laws were primarily written in Leviticus and Deuteronomy for Israelites residing in the Promised Land during the Old Covenant. Instead, they looked to laws given in Torah (1) for Gentiles *(goyim,* non-Jews, non-Hebrews, or non-Israelites/non-Israelis) constituting "the nations" outside of Israel as well as (2) for Gentiles residing in Israel as "foreigners," "sojourners," and "strangers" *(gerim* or resident aliens).

Laws written in Torah for Gentiles are known as Noahide (or Noachide) Laws because, after the flood, Noah became the primogenitor of all Gentiles through his sons and their progeny (i.e., through all of Ham's descendants, all of Japheth's descendants, and most of Shem's descendants).

To be a Noahide Christian during *the Millennium* meant to be a righteous Gentile: (1) who believes in Jesus Christ as the only-begotten Son of *God the Father* and Lord of lords; (2) who maintains his or her righteousness by abstaining from unholy thoughts, feelings, ideas, associations, images, affiliations, desires, deeds, words, attitudes, actions, and motives; and (3) who adheres to the Seven Noahide Laws. Derived, inferred, and extrapolated from Torah in conjunction with the Babylonian Talmud, these Seven Noahide Laws were used throughout *the Millennium* in the following iteration:

1. Recognize that Jesus Christ (Yeshua H'Moschiach or Yahoshuah Adonai) should be obeyed because he is Deity. If you do not obey him, then a penalty will be exacted from you. *Genesis 2:16*

2. Do not blaspheme, insult, ridicule, or curse the Creator-God's Name. If you use the Creator-God's Name in vain, then a penalty will be exacted from you. *Leviticus 24:15*

3. You must not shed innocent blood in the murder of another human being. If you murder someone, then a penalty will be exacted from you. *Genesis 9:6*

4. You should remain faithful to one lifelong spouse (a) by granting your spouse priority above all others and (b) by abstaining from sexual activity and romantic involvement with others. If you do not remain faithful to your spouse regarding these matters, then a penalty will be exacted from you. *Genesis 2:24; Acts 15:20 & 29*

5. Do not take what does not belong to you without permission or a penalty will be exacted from you. *Genesis 2:16-17 and 21:25-26*

6. Do not eat the blood of a living animal. In addition, when slaughtering animals for food, they should be drained completely of their blood. Blood from slaughtered animals should never be consumed by human beings except in trace amounts. *Genesis 9:4-5; Acts 15:20 & 29*

7. Establish local courts of law and justice to create formal ways and means of (a) evaluating infractions of these laws and (b) exacting penalties for disobeying them.

The Gentile-related laws stated above were deemed the most important although others existed in Torah *(for example,* in Genesis 9:1, 3, & 7; Exodus 12:43, 29:33, 30:33; Leviticus 16:25, 17:12, 18:26, 22:10-13 & 25, 24:22; Numbers 9:14, 15:16; and Deuteronomy 5:14).

Although the definition for a Noahide Christian during *the Millennium* was given earlier as incorporating three major characteristics, these additional characteristics are stated here to help resolve possible misconceptions:

1. Noahide Christians during *the Millennium* were Gentile followers and worshipers of Christ Jesus who adhered to the Seven Noahide Laws.

2. **Noahide Christians during *the Millennium* were not fixated on rules, regulations, and ordinances found in Torah.**

3. Noahide Christians during *the Millennium* were able to grasp the whole concept of Deity intellectually, emotionally, and spiritually while simultaneously attending to Deity's synchronized threeness (i.e., the Creator-God's tri-unity).

4. Noahide Christians during *the Millennium* did not reject any mainstream Christian doctrines associated with the unique birth, life, murder, resurrection, ascension, and Deity of *God the Son.*

5. Noahide Christians during *the Millennium* did not adhere to any written Old Testament legalism or invent any New Testament legalism.

6. Noahide Christians during *the Millennium* did not think of themselves, or present themselves to others, as pseudo-Jews, pseudo-Hebrews, or pseudo-Israelites.

Author's Note: An earlier iteration of the Seven Noahide Laws had been formally referenced by the 102nd Congress of the United States of America on March 20, 1991 in Public Law 102-14, a facsimile copy of which follows on the next two pages. In the document, Congress made clear that civilization would return to chaos if the Earth's inhabitants did not follow the letter of the Seven Noahide Laws, which return indeed happened before *the Millennium* as demonstrated through worldwide anarchy, lawlessness, criminality, and idolatry.

Public Law 102–14
102d Congress

Joint Resolution

Mar. 20, 1991
[H.J. Res. 104]

To designate March 26, 1991, as "Education Day, U.S.A.".

Whereas Congress recognizes the historical tradition of ethical values and principles which are the basis of civilized society and upon which our great Nation was founded;

Whereas these ethical values and principles have been the bedrock of society from the dawn of civilization, when they were known as the Seven Noahide Laws;

Whereas without these ethical values and principles the edifice of civilization stands in serious peril of returning to chaos;

Whereas society is profoundly concerned with the recent weakening of these principles that has resulted in crises that beleaguer and threaten the fabric of civilized society;

Whereas the justified preoccupation with these crises must not let the citizens of this Nation lose sight of their responsibility to transmit these historical ethical values from our distinguished past to the generations of the future;

Whereas the Lubavitch movement has fostered and promoted these ethical values and principles throughout the world;

Whereas Rabbi Menachem Mendel Schneerson, leader of the Lubavitch movement, is universally respected and revered and his eighty-ninth birthday falls on March 26, 1991;

Whereas in tribute to this great spiritual leader, "the rebbe", this, his ninetieth year will be seen as one of "education and giving", the year in which we turn to education and charity to return the world to the moral and ethical values contained in the Seven Noahide Laws; and

Whereas this will be reflected in an international scroll of honor signed by the President of the United States and other heads of state: Now, therefore, be it

Resolved by the Senate and House of Representatives of the United States of America in Congress assembled, That March 26,

1991, the start of the ninetieth year of Rabbi Menachem Schneerson, leader of the worldwide Lubavitch movement, is designated as "Education Day, U.S.A.". The President is requested to issue a proclamation calling upon the people of the United States to observe such day with appropriate ceremonies and activities.

Approved March 20, 1991.

LEGISLATIVE HISTORY—H.J. Res. 104:

CONGRESSIONAL RECORD, Vol. 137 (1991):
   Mar. 5, considered and passed House.
   Mar. 7, considered and passed Senate.

○

Resolution of Internal Conflicts during the Millennium

During *the Millennium,* children as well as adults learned how to recognize self-centered thoughts and feelings generated by their human flesh, and the carnal mind that directs it, as sometimes-powerful and often-cyclic distractions, intrusions, and nuisances that were not to be acted upon. At the same time, without being nonchalant about such self-centered thoughts and feelings, they were also taught neither to be ashamed nor guilt-ridden because they had such thoughts and feelings. And they were taught how to replace these thoughts and feelings with thoughts and feelings of a higher order by praying, meditating on God's written word in the Holy Bible, and refocusing their attention on "whatsoever things are true, whatsoever things are honest, whatsoever things are just, whatsoever things are pure, whatsoever things are lovely, and whatsoever things are of good report" (Philippians 4:8 KJV). This is how internal conflicts were handled during *the Millennium.* Interpersonal conflicts were handled through prayer, spiritual counselling, and local governance.

What Distinguished Souls Included in the First Resurrection?

Souls part of *the first resurrection* included:

Old Testament saints who: (1) had faith in the God of Abraham, Isaac, and Jacob; (2) helped prepare the way for the prophesied Messiah; and (3) believed on the expected Messiah either before he was born or while he was living on Earth. (The three faith-based criteria just stated are not mutually exclusive.)

New Testament saints who (1) accepted Christ Jesus as their personal Savior and Savior of the world and (2) believed on his (a) atoning sacrifice through crucifixion, (b) resurrection from the dead, (c) bodily ascension to Heaven, (d) lordship, and (e) deity.

After *the first resurrection* and during *the Millennium,* people living on Earth no longer belonged to the category of New Testament saints because their personal righteousness was no longer solely determined by believing on the remission of sins and reconciliation with God through the crucifixion of Christ Jesus (1 Corinthians 15:1-4). That dispensation (i.e., exemption from penalty for personal iniquity and sins based on one's heartfelt belief and profession of faith in Christ Jesus) ended when Christ Jesus returned to Earth as its sole Sovereign. For that reason, during *the Millennium,* righteousness was not just subsumed in faith and belief but also in honorable living, works, and sacrificial offerings to God.

Having been in *the first resurrection* was an unparalleled blessing because souls included were guaranteed a place in Eternity without the possibility of future judgment, condemnation, or separation from Deity. When the doubting Apostle Thomas saw the wounds of the resurrected Christ, he proclaimed: "My Lord and my God!" and Christ Jesus responded: "Blessed are those who have not seen and yet have believed" (John 20:29 KJV). Before *the Millennium,* salvation and resurrection were based only on the faith-based acceptance of the lordship, deity, and atoning sacrifice of Christ Jesus. During *the Millennium,* fulfilling that single criterion was no longer sufficient for redemption or *the second resurrection* at the end of *the Millennium* because the lordship, deity, and role of Christ Jesus was clearly visible to all living on Earth during that time. (Faith and hope in unseen truth do not exist when one can accede to truth based on what is irrefutably visible to all.)

To summarize, the dispensation of grace through faith in Jesus Christ ended when he returned to Earth to exercise his sovereignty.

Chapter Four

The Role of Free Will in Our Original Demise: Part One

When immortal beings were originally created, they were created without wrinkle, spot, or blemish. In other words, the souls and somatic identities (i.e., bodies) of immortal beings were perfect at the time of their creation. Paradoxically, although they were perfect, all newly-created immortal beings had an inherent latent flaw by design. This flaw was knowingly permitted by the Creator, but newly-created immortal beings were nonetheless perfect because the flaw had not yet been expressed, activated, or apparent at the time they were created. Their flaw, or weakness, would only become expressed, activated, and apparent when they reached a pressure level that originated from an interaction of specific pressures inside and outside of them: Their internal pressure came from desiring something that had been expressly forbidden by their Creator; and their external pressure came from being tempted by another consciousness — the consciousness of the fallen Lucifer, who had become *the Satan,* or eternal Adversary, of the Lord God Almighty.

This inherent latent flaw within these newly-created beings was not expressed, activated, or apparent until they chose to act on the combined pressure from their inner desire and an outer temptation. They chose to rebel against their Creator because of their own inner desire to know both good and evil coupled with Satan's specific temptation for them to act on that desire. (The

Creator alone is capable of knowing both good and evil at the same time without committing a sinful act. Immortal created beings needed to commit a sinful act in order for them to know both good and evil.)

In some ways, Adam and Eve wanted to be lied to by Satan in order to have an excuse for experiencing what had been forbidden by their Creator. The internal pressure from their own desire to err in combination with the external pressure from the temptation of Satan produced just the right level of pressure for their threshold of tolerance to be exceeded as created beings. Just as a perfectly cut diamond fractures when pressure placed upon it is ratcheted up to its breaking point, the perfect state of *immortal being* gifted to these newly-created immortals was fractured as a result of the combined pressures from their own errant desire and Satan's temptation. Their resulting action, trespass, and rebellion against the spoken command of the Creator-God demonstrated their inherent latent flaw.

Yes, the Creator knew of this flaw before He created us, but He wanted immortal beings at the time of their creation to receive the greatest gift He could possibly give: the gift of free will. He wanted His newly-created beings to be thoroughly created in His complete image and perfect likeness — which required that they have the same free will that He has. Thus was their inherent flaw by design and not by accident. Without practice and experimentation, the only *being* fit to have free will without the possibility of an errant incident is the Creator-God. Fortunately, through the shed blood of Christ Jesus, saved fallen beings have now been made fit to possess free will. And because their acceptance of that blood is an eternal decision, saved fallen created beings will never again fracture and fall through a spiritual rift after they are returned to their heavenly home (i.e., Heaven, Paradise, or Eden).

Their acceptance of salvation demonstrates that saved souls are deserving of free will. In contrast, their rejection of salvation demonstrates that unsaved souls are undeserving of free will.

>>>>><<<<<

Roundabout Number Four

God is defined in many ways in the Holy Bible. That *God* is referred to as "God of gods" in the Holy Bible (Deuteronomy 10:17; Joshua 22:22; Psalm 136:2; Daniel 2:47 and 11:36) does not mean that He is God of, over, or above other supreme beings but that He is God over other immortal beings (i.e., the "gods" from the phrase "God of gods"). In the Holy Bible, various related Hebrew words from which the word *gods* has been translated each have these multiple usages: (1) "the one true and only real God," (2) "false gods," (3) "pagan gods," (4) "idols" (statues of false or pagan gods), and (5) "immortal beings." Biblical context determines the actual definition of each Hebrew word when and where it is used. For the sake of clarity, the phrase *immortal beings* (i.e., *immortals*) is referring to incorporeal, unfallen created beings, each having a soul, higher order consciousness, free will, and a spiritual body (i.e., an *astral gelatinous*™ somatic identity).

The one true and only real *God* is sovereign and supreme above all other beings because He is *the Creator*. All other beings collectively constitute *the created*. Newly-created beings of the Adamic Race were immortal in Eden before their rebellion, fracture, and fall; and they were glorious — that is, enwrapped by the Creator's divine Light, heavenly Glory, or living Fire — before they acted on the desire to know both good and evil. In contrast, fallen created beings are no longer immortal: they are mortal. To be sure, the souls of all fallen created beings remain *eternal,* but they are not *immortal* today unless they are saved (more about that in Chapter Five). The view that unfallen immortal beings are referred to as "gods" in the Holy Bible is supported by many passages, including the following:

> I have said: "*You are gods* ["gods" here translated from the Hebrew word *elohim,* meaning "immortal beings"], and all of you are children of the Most High, but you shall die like men [i.e., mortals]..."
> *Psalm 82:6-7a KJV Paraphrase*

> Jesus replied to them, "Is it not written in your law, 'I have said: *You are gods*'"?
> *John 10:34 KJV Paraphrase*

The word *gods* in the two passages just cited, as well as in many other places in the Holy Bible, does not mean "little deities" or "created beings who deserve to be worshiped." In this context, the word *gods* means "immortal, or unfallen, created beings" (i.e., immortals) in contrast to "mortal, or fallen, created beings" (i.e., mortals).

"Adam and Eve" have multiple meanings in the Genesis account of creation: (1) "Adam and Eve" represent the unfallen spiritual beings collectively referred to as the Adamic Race, who were newly-created immortal beings in the Garden of Eden (i.e., Paradise or Heaven). (2) "Adam and Eve" represent the fallen created beings collectively referred to as the fallen Adamic Race and individually known as mortal beings, mortals, or human beings. And (3) "Adam and Eve" represent two specific people who were: (a) expelled from the Garden of Eden; (b) transformed from immortals to mortals (i.e., from life to death) as a result of their rebellion, fracture, fall, and expulsion; and (c) charged with populating the Earth.

End of Roundabout Number Four

The Role of Free Will in Our Original Demise: Part Two

Free will had an inherent latent flaw for newly-created immortal beings because they did not have the experience to use free will correctly. Unlike the Creator — who was, is, and always will be able to handle His own free will without practice and experimentation — newly-created beings were unable to handle their own free will without practice or experimentation. The Creator knew this before He created the unfallen Adamic Race. Free will is too huge for newly-created beings to handle without their making mistakes. Like learning how to ride a bicycle, newly-created beings needed to learn how to navigate using free will through practice and experimentation.

With practice and experimentation, new bicyclists learn from their mistakes in order to make right choices in successive attempts at bicycle riding. Similarly, newly-created beings must learn from their mistakes in order to become highly-skilled in using free will correctly and effectively. Created beings must learn to make right choices in order to please the Creator-God as well as not disappoint themselves. All fallen created beings are capable of learning, but not all fallen created beings choose to apply what they have learned. Some choose to become sour, bitter, and salty in their attitudes and temperaments. Some choose to please themselves at the expense of pleasing their Creator, for which sole purpose all of us were originally created.

When created beings first chose to please themselves rather than please their Creator, they fell through a vortical rift from their pristine state of original being to *the state of being* known as *mortality*. The Adamic Race of newly-created beings sought to place themselves on *equal footing with* their Creator. In contrast, Lucifer had sought to exalt himself *above* the Creator. Although redemption is not possible for Lucifer and the angels who subordinated themselves to him, redemption is still possible for members of the fallen Adamic Race through their individual repentance and acceptance of the shed blood of Jesus Christ as the only atoning sacrifice acceptable to the Creator-God for the remission of their iniquity and sins and the cancellation of the debt they owe to Him for their iniquity and sins.

Please be advised that words like "mistake," "errant action," and "trespass" are lightweight descriptors when used to represent sin, rebellion, and the voluntary decision to violate the commandments of God. Except for blasphemy against God's Holy Spirit and the conscious, informed decision to eternally reject the *only-begotten* Son of God (both of which merit damnation because they cannot be forgiven), all sin is sin regardless of what lightweight descriptors might be used to label it. In this communication, alternate word choices for "sin" are not intended to take away from the hideous, vulgar, and evil nature of sin.

In summary, when souls with free will were originally created, they did not know how to navigate through life because they really did not know how to keep free will in check without ever having practiced or experimented with it in difficult circumstances. To be sure, in our original status as immortals, we were inexperienced. This inexperience with free will brought about our own demise and the current mortal state in which you (the reader or listener) find yourselves. However, as I can personally attest, once one is fully restored to Heaven, one is no longer subject to: (1) lustful desires or (2) temptations.

The Where and When of Eden

The terms *Heaven, Paradise,* and *Eden* are all synonymous because they all represent the pristine eternal abode of the Creator-God and His unfallen creation. Although there are those who would like to distinguish these three terms from one another as each representing a different state, location, or place, all of them represent the same eternal state of glorious being.

Eternal beings were created in *Eden,* the unblemished Garden of the Creator-God. When they disobeyed the Will of the Creator-God, it was they who changed and not *Eden. Eden* remained intact and unchanged. It was they who were expelled from *Eden.* It was they whose glory was darkened. It was they who ceased to exist in a pristine eternity. It was they who widened a rift in eternity through their disobedience to the Will of the Creator-God. Metaphysically speaking, it was the Luciferian Fall that originally caused the outpocketing from eternity that became temporality (see Figure One on page 72); the Adamic Fall simply widened that rift.

Temporality was born in the first act of disobedience to the Will of the Creator-God. And that first act of disobedience by Lucifer corresponds to the chaotic origin of the physical universe in its *Big Bang.* The physical universe does not exist in eternity, and eternity does not exist in the physical universe. Concomitantly, temporality does not exist in eternity, and eternity does not exist in temporality. The physical universe has a beginning and an ending, and its temporality has a beginning and an ending. The spiritual universe does not have a beginning or an ending, and its eternity does not have a beginning or an ending. The abode of the Creator-God is neither in the physical universe nor in temporality. The Creator-God and all unfallen created beings, as well as all souls restored to immortality, reside in eternity.

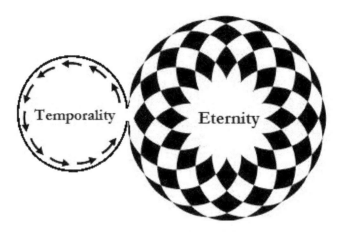

The Outpocketing of Temporality from Eternity

Figure One

For the sake of clarification, *the whole Universe* consisted only of eternity before the origin of iniquity and the *Big Bang*. During the seven thousand years of Biblical history (from Genesis to the creation of "a new heaven and a new earth" at the end of *the Millennium), the whole Universe* consisted of both eternity and temporality. At the end of *the Millennium, the whole Universe* again consists only of eternity. Because I am writing to you from 3050 AD, I am writing to you from eternity. Temporality no longer exists in 3050 AD. Temporality ceased to exist at the end of *the Millennium.*

All disobedient immortals fell from eternity through the rift that was created into *their* newly-formed state of mortality, which has both visible and invisible realms (i.e., corporeal and incorporeal modes). Although all errant beings retained their eternal — albeit tainted — souls, they became enmeshed in the skeins of relative space-time in temporality. Although eternity has neither a beginning nor an ending, temporality does have a beginning and an ending (hence the direction of arrows in Figure One). As a side note for anyone who sees conceptual flaws in Figure One: all metaphysical symbology, in words as well as in images, is flawed because it can only represent a few relational aspects of timeless and dimensionless spiritual truth.

Eden has always existed and will continue to exist in its pristine state; and a pristine state has always existed and will continue to exist in *Eden*. Temporality, however, cannot exist in *Eden,* and *Eden* cannot exist in temporality. Physicality (i.e., the physical universe) is found in temporality; physicality is not found in eternity. Temporality is one part of *the whole Universe,* but temporality is not part of eternity. Temporality is found only in physicality (i.e., corporeal mortality) and its associated invisible realm (i.e., incorporeal mortality). Although Hell *(Hades* or *Sheol)* is an incorporeal condition, mode, or realm of being in the state of mortality, it is considered a part of temporality because its existence is of a specified — and, therefore, *temporal*— duration.

To be sure, time in physicality can be measured and quantified. Although an eternal soul can inhabit a human body and, therefore, sojourn in temporality, the eternal soul itself does not obey the laws of chronological time. The physical body that the eternal soul indwells does obey the laws of chronological time, but its eternal soul does not. If you live in a house on Earth, you would never confuse yourself with your house. You would simply understand that it is the place where you live. The same should be true concerning your human body. However, because many misconclude that they *are* their human bodies, they never pause to discover their souls. They neither look outside in nor inside out.

Physical time, which is measured quantitatively in temporality, is not *spiritual time,* which is measured qualitatively in eternity. *Physical time* has various bends, creases, folds, bridges, cracks, and holes in its skeins, creating numerous relative periods of chronological time. Even though numerous relative periods of physical time exist, and even though they are all interconnected in one way or another, none of these periods of time are continuous with — or connected to — eternity. Although there is no bend, crease, fold, or bridge in temporality that leads to eternity, there is a vortical rift in eternity that leads to temporality. In general, eternity exists separately from temporality. Again, the existence of temporality is the effect of eternal souls who disobeyed the Will of the Creator-God. Disobedience to the Will of the Creator-God resulted in created beings falling into temporality. At the end of *the Millennium,* temporality (relative space-time) will cease to exist because it will be swallowed up, engulfed, and reabsorbed by eternity (absolute space-time) when the Creator-God infuses the entire physical universe with the Totality of His Fiery Being.

Spiritual time is action-based. *Spiritual time* is qualified but not quantified. In *spiritual time,* events occur in the *now.* The *now* is where we are when we are fully returned to eternity through our belief in Christ Jesus as Lord and Savior. The *now* is an ever-present reality. Although I have stated that I am writing to you from 3050 AD, there really is no 3050 AD in eternity. I am actually writing to you from the *now* of eternity, but I wanted to provide you (the reader or listener) with a referent (i.e., something to which you could relate). The non-existent year 3050 AD is your referent. (Although this is somewhat humorous to me, I did not endeavor to have a laugh at your expense.)

I am writing to you from a place where temporality no longer exists. All temporality ceased to exist upon the formation of "a new heaven and a new earth" — which formation is a metaphor for the passing away of temporality through its dissolution into, and resorption by, eternity. At the time of the formation of "a new heaven and a new earth," all relative space-time ceased to exist, and the Creator-God's restored creation was fully infused by His divine Light, heavenly Glory, or living Fire. At that instant, the physical universe ceased to exist: Temporality was overtaken and engulfed by eternity. And, of course, *Death* and *Hades* no longer exist. Except for those unsaved fallen beings relegated to *the Lake of Fire,* all other fallen beings are now fully restored to their original pristine state of *astral gelatinous*™ being and are eternally reunited with the Creator-God because they accepted Christ Jesus as their eternal Lord and Savior.

On Being One with the Creator-God

Total immersion in the light, love, and life of the Creator-God can be daunting to most human beings who treasure their individuality and personal freedom. As someone who was remarkably headstrong, willful, and full of woeful pride, I certainly was afraid of losing myself in physical death. However, as I died, I found that there is nothing to lose and everything to gain when one *falls asleep in Jesus.*

When I died, I went directly to be with the Lord Jesus Christ in Heaven. Now Heaven may be a state without the place, but it is never a place without the state — the state of living, moving, and being in Christ Jesus. Heaven is the state of *total immersion* in the light, love, and life of our Lord Jesus Christ. Here, the phrase *total immersion* is used in contrast to the phrase *complete infusion.* *Complete infusion* of the physical universe with the spiritual supramolecules and divine Fire of the Creator-God's Sovereign and Supreme Being takes place at the end of *the Millennium* (reread 1

Corinthians 15:24-28 in Chapter One of this book) — after the Great White Throne Judgment of God. *Total immersion* in the light, love, and life of our Lord Jesus Christ occurs for every Christian the moment that his or her physical body dies.

As soon as I died, I met many of my family and friends who had preceded me in death. Because the Lord Jesus had not yet returned to Earth, none of the saved dead I met had received their new somatic identities. Instead, they presented themselves in facsimiles of the *vehicles* in which they travelled either when they were last on Earth or during the periods of time on Earth that represented their greatest contentment. However, my recognition of them did not depend on how they appeared. Because recognition comes from inside one's soul in Heaven, it is based on communication from soul to soul and not on how one views outer appearances. In short, I knew who each person was immediately — even though some looked quite different from when I knew them or how I remembered them. In many ways, the human body is a chrysalis for the soul because its inherent carnal nature is an opposing force that causes us to make a choice between right or wrong, good or evil, and pleasing our Creator or displeasing Him. (The word *causes* is used here in a metaphysical sense and is analogous to environmental factors that stimulate a seed to germinate or a flower bud to bloom.)

Although I was greeted warmly and lovingly by my family and friends who were already in Heaven, I felt a sense of urgency to meet the one who had died for my iniquity and sin — the one to whom I owed everything. One of my spiritual mentors stepped forward and advised me that she would be ushering me to the throne room of the King of kings. Along the way, she thanked me for some of the matters that I had tended to while I was on Earth. I told her that I could not have accomplished what I did without her help, without the help of others, and without the blessing of our

Lord Jesus Christ. Immediately after I thanked her, we were at the door to the throne room. I was dizzy with excitement and could scarcely believe that this moment had arrived.

Suddenly, my mentor disappeared and the door to the throne room opened and I could see a dazzling brilliant light emanating from a throne of gold and silver. I could see the details of the throne even through its brilliant light. I became instantly aware of each symbol engraved on the throne and its profound significance. I then came face to face with the Savior of the world standing at the throne. As soon as I saw the Savior I was reminded of the charming legend about red roses that I had learned as a child: The legend is that all roses were white until Christ Jesus was slain. Then, the roses blushed red with shame when they apprehended the purity of the Savior. Indeed, I was struck by the purity of our Savior's being. His purity was whiter and brighter than anything I had ever imagined when I was a human being.

There was no need for either of us to introduce ourselves to each other. We each knew fully well who the other was.

Roundabout Number Five

Because it is so very easy for created beings in a fallen state to confuse themselves with the Creator-God (you do it all the time), I will now take a detour to discuss the answer to the question that each one of you should pose to yourself: "How do I — the reader or listener — know that I am *not* the Creator-God?"

Hopefully, your thoughtful answer will include at least some aspects of each of the nine assumptions that follow:

1. I am *not* the Creator-God because I am a created being. The Creator-God alone is Self-Existent and, therefore, is the only Being that exists who has not been created.

2. I am *not* the Creator-God because, although I channel His light, love, and life, I am not the source of that light, love, and life.

3. I am *not* the Creator-God because I do not deserve to be worshiped and because I will never deserve to be worshiped. The Creator-God alone deserves to be worshiped.

4. I am *not* the Creator-God because, although I have creative energies within me, I am not the originator of those energies. I merely channel those energies.

5. I am *not* the Creator-God because my will needs to conform to His Will, and His Will does not need to conform to my will. As a created being, although I have been gifted with my own personal volition and self-awareness, my own personal volition was not given for me to disobey the Will of God and my own self-awareness was not given for me to exalt it over anyone else, at any level, ever.

6. I am *not* the Creator-God because I only know in part, and I will always only know in part; only the Creator-God has known, knows, and will know everything all at once.

7. I am *not* the Creator-God because I am not everywhere, and I will never be everywhere; only the Creator-God was, is, and will be everywhere.

8. I am *not* the Creator-God because I do not have all power and authority; only the Creator-God has had, currently has, and will always have all power and authority.

9. I am *not* the Creator-God because I always have had, now have, and always will have limitations regardless of changes to the

parameters of those limitations, and regardless of whether I am on Earth or in the Paradise of God known as *Heaven*.

A piece of a cardboard puzzle cannot say: "I made myself!" or "I constitute the whole puzzle!" And neither can any created being say: "I created myself!" or "I constitute the entirety of God's creation!"

In contrast to the previous nine assumptions, here is what a created being who is fallen believes (erroneously, of course):

1. I am responsible for whatever success I have attained. Others are responsible for whatever success I have been denied.

2. Others benefit because I exist. I am the source of their joy and comfort. Others rest securely only because I exist.

3. I expect recognition because I deserve recognition. I expect others to credit me for my contributions to their well-being. Any bitterness that I now have is justified because I have not received the recognition and credit I deserve.

4. I am the source of my own gifts, talents, skills, and abilities. I do not owe my success to anyone other than me.

5. Others need to obey and execute my will because my will is superior to the will of all others.

6. I am superior to all others in wisdom and understanding. I know better than everyone else. No one is able to teach me anything that I don't already know.

7. I will go where I want to go and no one can stop me.

8. I am better than others because I am superior to others.

9. I am without limitations. There are no boundaries to what I can, and will, achieve.

In effect, all unsaved fallen beings believe that they have created themselves. And, to the extent that a fallen being is responsible for the hideous distortion of its original self, there is a modicum of truth to that belief.

Even if you — the reader or listener — deny it, you still operate daily as if the second set of nine statements is true regardless of whether you are the weakest member of a street gang or the chief executive officer of a large corporation. How do I know that? I know that because you are fallen. That is what fallen beings think and how they act regardless of where they are. Even if you are a saved fallen being, you are still pulled in the direction of assuming that the second set of nine statements is true. If you still exist in corporeality, saved or unsaved, you cannot help but think, at least periodically, that the second set of statements is true. However, when you are saved, another voice can also be heard within you that reminds you of your divine nature now that you are saved.

Even some Christians living in your generation demonstrate that they believe that the second set of statements is true. They believe that all they need to do is speak what they want and they will receive it without regard to the needs of others and without regard to the Will of the Creator-God or His timing. They believe that any discord, pain, or suffering within their lives is a sign that either they have a lack of faith or that they have not used the right spoken formula to release the Creator-God's goodness upon themselves. By their actions, they demonstrate that they either think they can play the role of the Creator-God or think that the Creator-God can be played (i.e., manipulated) with the right spoken formula. Attempting to *speak things into existence* by human beings is mostly a sign of gross spiritual immaturity.

End of Roundabout Number Five

The Appearance of the Lord Jesus Christ

When I first saw the Lord Jesus Christ, both he and I were engulfed in his divine Light (heavenly Glory or living Fire). His heavenly Glory is a brilliant white light that billows from him in clouds, each cloud containing a fine mist of the living supramolecules and divine Fire of the Creator-God's Holy Spirit (please be reminded that the supramolecules and fire are spiritual and not physical). The clouds of his divine Light emanate from his Being, and his heavenly Glory is so intense that it penetrated my own being like the power of 100 million locomotives passing through me all at once. At the same time, I felt the height, depth, and breadth of his Supraconsciousness and I knew it to be wildly superior to the minds of all created beings, individually as well as collectively. I knew that there never was, or ever could be, anyone like him, the one and only spoken Word of God.

I saw divine Life within him and I was impressed by its tangibility and spiritually substantive nature. I saw living beings projected within him almost like swarms of bees, schools of fish, or murmurations of birds swirling and darting to and fro in unison, their vortical patterns profoundly proclaiming him, in pulsating fashion, to be the author of all life, of all created beings, and of all living creatures throughout the entire expanse of the Creator-God's unending *Universe*.

I also saw and felt divine Love radiating from the inner core of his Being. As the rays of his love penetrated my being, I was comforted, nurtured, welcomed, warmed, encouraged, protected, reassured, embraced, dandled, forgiven, healed, anointed, and actualized all at the same time.

The Savior was clothed in a pure white garment composed of shimmering silver and golden threads configured into a brocade pattern that had a holographic *alto relief* appearance. This pattern included beautiful ornamentation in blue, purple, and scarlet as well as floating inscriptions — sometimes intersecting as they moved, sometimes not — of all the names by which he had been called in the Holy Bible (*for example,* "the Bright and Morning Star," "the Lamb of God," "the Lion of Judah," "the Word of God," and "the Rose of Sharon"). However, one of his names was in indecipherable glyphic characters that no one could read, utter, or know the meaning of but he himself. (There is always a part of the Creator-God unknowable to created beings!)

Upon his head was a golden crown that had emblazoned on it in a decipherable heavenly language: "Holiness to *the Name!*" — which is instantly understood by all to mean: "Holiness to *Yahweh,* the Lord God Almighty!"

The person of the Christ was *astral gelatinous*™ in nature (reread *Roundabout Number Two* in Chapter One). As such, his somatic identity possessed its own intrinsic luminosity that continually emanated spiritual light, which light did not abate in brilliance because of its continuous emission. The most noticeable of all of his facial features were his eyes because they were aflame with a penetrating light of supernova intensity.

When the Savior spoke to me, it was like the sound of many waters skipping, babbling, and clapping on the stones in a river. At the very same time, his voice thundered ominously with peals of lightening and laughter. His words were like pearls that dropped from his mouth, bouncing in space to penetrate and integrate themselves into my own being. I saw a different colored gemstone in my mind with each word that he spoke. The brilliance of every gemstone simultaneously imparted the height, depth, and breadth of each word's multiple meanings.

At first, in awe of his unparalleled majesty and beauty, I stood transfixed by his glorious presence. Then, involuntarily and reflexively: my arms instantly became elevated and outstretched, I fell on my knees and lower legs, and my head bowed down toward him. Although when I was on Earth I had believed in my heart and confessed with my mouth that he was my Lord and Savior, for the first time I now proclaimed my oath of eternal fealty to him. At this moment, I indentured myself to him eternally and, as a result, I learned the true extent of my personal freedom as his joint heir.

Chapter Five

States and Conditions of Being

In this book, the words *immortality* and *mortality* describe states of being. And the words *corporeality* and *incorporeality* describe conditions, modes, or realms of being.

Created souls that live, move, and have their being in immortality are *immortals,* or *immortal beings.* Immortals exist as unfallen beings in Heaven and as saved fallen beings either on Earth or in Heaven. (In other words, human beings regain an immortal status immediately when they are saved.) Unfallen beings in Heaven are always incorporeal; saved fallen beings in Heaven have been restored to incorporeality; but saved fallen beings on Earth are still in corporeality. Because saved fallen beings still in corporeality have a dual nature (i.e., both a divine nature and a carnal, or flesh, nature), their souls live, move, and have their being in immortality at the same time that their human bodies exist in the corporeal realm of mortality. Thus, the souls of saved fallen beings in corporeality are immortal but their bodies are corporeal and mortal. In keeping with the definition of immortality used in this book, all saved fallen beings, regardless of whether they are in corporeality or in incorporeality, are in the state of being that is known as *immortality.*

Unsaved fallen souls that live, move, and have their being in mortality are *mortals,* or *mortal beings.* Mortals exist in mortality either as unsaved fallen beings in corporeality (i.e., as incarnates) or as unsaved fallen beings in incorporeality (i.e., as discarnates). In keeping with the definition of mortality used in this book, all unsaved fallen beings, regardless of whether they are in corporeality or in incorporeality, are in the state of being that is known as *mortality*.

Incorporeal *mortals* have nothing in common with incorporeal *immortals* except for their incorporeality and the eternal nature of their souls. *Mortals* are fallen and unsaved regardless of whether they are corporeal or incorporeal. *Immortals* are either unfallen (*for example,* as heavenly angels) or restored to immortality because their souls are saved (regardless of whether their somatic identities are corporeal or incorporeal).

Because incorporeal beings do not have a physical body, they are invisible to the overwhelming majority of human beings regardless of whether the human beings are saved or unsaved. However, there is a rare category of human beings who occasionally hear and/or see incorporeal beings, and they are known to those of us in Heaven as *susceptible channels*.

Multiple Meanings of *Death*

The word *death* has multiple meanings in the Holy Bible. Sometimes the multiple meanings are expressed simultaneously by the word. And sometimes only a single meaning is expressed by the word. The meaning of *death* in the Holy Bible depends on: (1) the context of the word's usage; (2) the limitations imposed on the word's meanings by the reader; and (3) the levels of meaning intended, implied, and permitted by God's Holy Spirit.

Four multiple meanings of the word *death* in the Holy Bible follow:

(1) *Death* can refer to a soul's passing from corporeality to incorporeality at the time that its inhabited human body permanently shuts down.

(2) *Death* can refer to the act of separation of a fallen being from the Creator-God by its iniquity and sin. Here, *iniquity* means "turning away from God" and *sin* means "action based on that turning."

(3) *Death* can refer to the state of being for fallen souls known as *mortality*. Thus, *death* can refer to *mortality* as an *effect* of one's fallen nature and separation from the Creator-God. As used in this book, *mortality* is a state of being that includes all unsaved souls in corporeality and all unsaved souls in incorporeality. Thus, *mortality* includes an incorporeal realm that is known as *Hell (Hades* or *Sheol)* in the Holy Bible. (Hell is covered in the next major section of this chapter.) As *the Lake of Fire* is also called *the second death* in the Holy Bible, so is *mortality* also called *the first death* in this book. *(The Lake of Fire* is described in the fourth major section of this chapter.) And, because *death* blankets invisible realities from those in the corporeal realm, corporeality can also be called (a) *the shadow of death* (where *death* refers to *mortality* as defined in this book) and (b) *the shadow of turning* (where *turning* refers to *iniquity* as defined in this book). As stated previously, all unsaved souls are *mortals* regardless of whether they are corporeal or incorporeal (i.e., regardless of whether they are incarnates or discarnates). In contrast, all saved souls are *immortals* regardless of whether they are corporeal or incorporeal (i.e., regardless of whether they are incarnates or discarnates).

(4) *Death* can refer to the specific realm, or level, in mortality that is named *corporeality* — where eternal souls are recycled in

human incarnations, or human lifetimes, until they make an informed, final decision to either eternally serve the Creator-God or permanently remain in rebellion against Him. However, as indicated previously, *corporeality* may be referred to as *the shadow of death* or *the shadow of turning* rather than just *death*. When *death* is referring to corporeality, it refers to a condition, mode, or realm of being rather than an entire state of being. In keeping with word usage in this book, *mortality* is a state of being and *corporeality* is a condition, mode, or realm of *mortality*.

To summarize two key points thus far: (1) mortality is *the state of being* known as *death* (i.e., *the first death),* where all unsaved souls, or mortals, dwell; and (2) some mortals are corporeal beings, and other mortals are incorporeal beings. In contrast, a saved soul is no longer *mortal* but *immortal* in the same way that a saved soul in Heaven is immortal. Thus, saved souls are immortals regardless of whether they are in a corporeal realm or in an incorporeal realm. To be sure, the human bodies of saved souls are in a corporeal condition even though their souls are in an immortal state. In other words, all saved souls are fully restored to immortality (although they may not be fully returned to Eden) regardless of where they are in *the whole Universe* and regardless of their individual somatic identities. (For the sake of clarity, the word *saved* here is referring to those who are authentically Christian.)

Fallen beings not only fell from eternity to temporality but, concomitantly, from the state of immortality in Eden to the state of mortality outside of Eden (such fall to mortality known as *the first death* in this book). The state of mortality for souls outside of Eden on the planet Earth predicates the condition of temporality (i.e., relative space-time) imposed upon them; this temporality is commonly measured by solar time, lunar time, sidereal time, and atomic clock time in corporeality. Such measured time is also referred to as *chronological time.*

As seen by immortals from eternity, both corporeal and incorporeal realms are found in the state of mortality. The realm of mortality visible to human beings is referred to as corporeality, and the realm of mortality invisible to human beings is referred to as incorporeality. Although all corporeality is a fallen realm within the state of mortality, not all incorporeality is a fallen realm within the state of mortality because incorporeality as a condition is also associated with immortals in eternity.

To further explain, saved souls were restored to their original pristine state by having been metaphysically passed through the shed blood of the Lord Jesus Christ at the precise moment that they accepted him as their personal Savior while they were on Earth as human beings. Even though their bodies exist in corporeality, their souls no longer live in mortality; their souls live in immortality.

To human beings, saved souls in Heaven are invisible and are, therefore, incorporeal.

To summarize an additional key point thus far: the souls of unsaved incorporeal beings live, move, and have their entire being in the state known as *mortality;* and the souls of saved incorporeal beings live, move, and have their entire being in the state known as *immortality.*

For the sake of clarity, because some important words, terms, and phrases in this book are not regularly used by many readers or listeners, reiteration and restatement are often employed by the present author to help the meanings of specific words, terms, phrases, and their inter-relationships make greater sense and, therefore, encourage readers and listeners to make the words a part of their thinking as well as a part of their active vocabularies.

As taught in the Holy Bible, the final victory for saved fallen souls will be over all forms of *death* (1 Corinthians 15:26). Thus, (1) there will be victory over *the grave* (i.e., physical death); (2) there will no longer be any separation from the Creator-God except for eternally-damned souls (i.e., the souls of the evil dead); (3) there will be complete removal of *the state of being* known as *mortality;* and (4) there will be victory over human flesh and the carnal mind that directs it. In short, when complete victory over *death* is achieved, there will be no physical death, no separation from the Creator-God (except for souls eternally damned), no mortality, and no corporeality.

As taught in Revelation 20:13-15, *Death* and *Hades* are eventually cast into *the Lake of Fire* along with: (1) all souls who are *devils, demons, unclean spirits,* or *evil spirits* (referred to as existing *in the sea* in Revelation 20:13 KJV); and (2) all souls in mortality (either in corporeality or in *Hades)* whose names are not written in *the Book of Life.* That Christ Jesus proclaimed that he himself had the "keys of *hell* and of *death"* (Revelation 1:18 KJV) means that only he possesses the power to release souls from: (1) *the state of being* known as *mortality,* (2) the realm of mortality known as corporeality, and (3) the realm of mortality known as Hades. (By *release,* I do not mean to imply that all souls will be saved or restored because, not only will all demons be released from the *bottomless pit of the Abyss in Hades* and be thrown into *the Lake of Fire* at the end of *the Millennium,* but also many of the souls released from the other levels of *Hades* as well as from corporeality will also be thrown into *the Lake of Fire* at the end of *the Millennium.)*

There is a distinction between *immortality* and *eternity* as the words are used in this discourse. Immortality is a state of being reserved only for the Creator, all unfallen beings (*for example,* unfallen angels), and all saved, or restored, souls. Eternity is the dimensionless reality that exists for all created beings, regardless of whether they are eternally redeemed in Heaven or eternally damned in *the Lake of Fire.* When all souls were created, they were created to be eternal — which is to say, their souls can never be extinguished, annihilated, or expunged. Thus, not only are souls eternal in the state of immortality, souls are eternal in mortality, in corporeality, and in *the Lake of Fire,* too. To reemphasize one key point in this paragraph, all souls are eternal regardless of where they are found in *the whole Universe* and regardless of their somatic identity. Following are some helpful summary statements with regard to eternity, immortality, mortality, and corporeality:

1. All souls are eternal, but all souls are not immortal.

2. All unsaved souls are mortal, but not all unsaved souls are corporeal.

3. All saved souls are immortal, but not all saved souls are incorporeal.

Previously in this section, I listed four multiple meanings for the word *death.* To help ensure that the reader or listener understands concepts associated with these alternate meanings, I will now provide examples of what the phrase *dead person* can mean, depending on Biblical context:

1. A *dead person* is someone whose human life has ended.

2. A *dead person* is someone who has been separated from the Creator-God by his or her rebellious nature.

3. A *dead person* is someone who is unsaved.

4. A *dead person* is someone whose soul fell from immortality to mortality.

5. A *dead person* is a *mortal* (i.e., someone who exists in the state of being that is known as *mortality).*

6. A *dead person* is someone who is unsaved and who lives in corporeality as an unsaved human being.

7. A *dead person* is someone who is unsaved and who exists in *Hades* as a discarnate.

8. Although all saints on Earth and in Heaven are *dead to sin* and *dead with Christ,* no saint who lives in Heaven as a redeemed soul or on Earth as a saved human being is really a *dead person.* That is one reason the Holy Bible uses the phrase "fallen asleep" to describe a saved person whose human life has ended: That person is not really dead because its life is ongoing. (Another reason is that a newly-deceased person, especially one who has just died of natural causes, appears to be asleep.)

Hell (Hades or Sheol)

Hell (Hades or *Sheol)* is a realm, or locus, of being for the souls of the unsaved dead. Here, the category of *unsaved dead* includes: (1) souls who will never be saved (i.e., the "eternally lost dead" or "evil dead"); and (2) souls who still have a chance for salvation up until the end of *the Millennium.* After *the Millennium,* Hell does not exist and there are no new opportunities for salvation. Hell does not exist after *the Millennium* because Hell itself gets thrown into *the Lake of Fire* at the end of *the Millennium* (Revelation 20:14). At the end of *the Millennium,* there are no new opportunities for salvation because the recycling of souls in human bodies ends when *the Millennium* ends. The end of (1) Hell and (2) all salvation opportunities occurs specifically at the time of the Great White Throne Judgment of the Creator-God.

As indicated earlier, although Hell is an incorporeal condition, mode, or realm of being in the state of mortality, it is considered a part of temporality because its existence is of a specified — and, therefore, *temporal* — duration.

Although Hell in certain English translations of the New Testament is sometimes associated with divine Fire, in most of those cases the word Hell has been translated from the Greek word *Gehenna* and not from the Greek word *Hades*. Thus, when Hell in the New Testament has been translated from *Gehenna,* it is generally referring to, or presaging, *the Lake of Fire* — which is discussed in the next major section of this chapter. (The phrase *the Lake of Fire* is used only in the Book of Revelation, which was written after all other texts in the New Testament.)

Discussion of Hell in this section is restricted to its use associated with the Greek word *Hades* and, occasionally, with the Hebrew word *Sheol. Sheol* is the Hebrew word that is translated as Hell in the Old Testament of the Holy Bible (KJV). However, *Sheol,* as used in the Old Testament, has the following multiple meanings: (1) grave, (2) abode of the dead, (3) holding tank for the dead, and (4) dungeon and place of no return for the exiled dead (i.e., *the pit).* To be sure, like many other words, the specific meaning for *Sheol* in the Old Testament depends on the context in which it is used.

Hell (Hades or Sheol) is the infernal abode of disembodied spirits, incorporeal beings, or discarnates who are not saved. When fallen souls were evicted from Eden because of their rebelliousness, the Creator-God consigned them to *the state of being* known as *mortality,* which includes both corporeality and Hell. At that time, the Creator-God decreed that a soul could receive salvation only while the soul was in corporeality (specifically in a human body during an earthly incarnation appointed by the Creator-God). Although it is not possible for souls to receive salvation when they are discarnates, some souls in Hell are still eligible for salvation and are, therefore, recycled in (i.e., released for) additional incarnations. However, not all souls in Hell (Hades or Sheol) are eligible for salvation opportunities in additional incarnations.

Because I am writing to you from 3050 AD, Hell (Hades or Sheol) no longer exists — every soul is already in a state of eternal redemption or in a state of eternal damnation. But I can tell you more about Hell's origin and who resided in its various levels when it did exist.

Hell (Hades or Sheol) is an incorporeal locus of mortal being that is invisible to souls in corporeality (i.e., invisible to incarnate beings) but visible to souls in incorporeality (i.e., visible to discarnate beings). As an incorporeal locus of mortal being, Hell was vocalized, articulated, and actualized into existence by the God of the Holy Bible at the time of temporality's initial outpocketing from eternity, which occurred the instant that iniquity and sin first existed. In elaborating the parameters for Hell, the God of the Holy Bible created a holding tank (with levels) for: (1) souls not yet saints, (2) souls that would never become saints but were not yet unclean spirits, and (3) souls that would be cast out of the earth plane of consciousness as unclean spirits. Concerning the third category, exorcised unclean spirits are cast into *the bottomless pit of the Abyss in Hades* (the lowest level of Hell), where the fallen angels referenced in Jude 1:6 also await their transfer to *the Lake of Fire* at the end of *the Millennium.*

Regardless of whether they lived during Old Testament times, during New Testament times, or during *the Millennium,* "saints" are people, living or dead, who desire to abide by the Will of the Creator-God. Such desire includes (1) their continuous acceptance of the Will of the Creator-God as well as (2) replacing their own desires with the desires of the Creator-God and (3) not doing what they want but, instead, what the Creator-God wants. Souls enter sainthood when they desire to be true to the Creator-God — not just for a moment but for all eternity.

Hell houses all souls that will be given additional opportunities for salvation, and Hell also houses demons.

Demons are also known as *devils, unclean spirits,* and *evil spirits* in different translations of the Holy Bible. The terms *demons, devils, unclean spirits,* and *evil spirits* may be used interchangeably because they are synonymous. In short, the souls of the unsaved dead that are eternally lost are demons, devils, unclean spirits, or evil spirits. In order to become an unclean spirit, a soul must make the conscious decision: (1) to always put its own will before the Will of the Creator-God, (2) to always put its own desires before the desires of the Creator-God, and (3) to always do what it wants to do and not what the Creator-God wants it to do. Demons are the discarnate souls of those who have made such conscious decisions either during their final incarnation on Earth or in incorporeality after they have died. The reason that the incarnation is "their final incarnation" is because the conscious decision to irrevocably disobey the Will of the Creator-God puts an end to future opportunities for additional lifetimes and, therefore, to future opportunities for salvation and for any and all spiritual advancement. When a discarnate is "unclean," it is beyond reclamation.

Discarnate souls not yet saints (i.e., not yet saved) dwell in the dimensionless reality of Hades awaiting reentrance to the earth plane of consciousness in additional human lifetimes, or human incarnations. That they will become saints is not yet known to them although it is known to the Creator-God. The Creator-God provides additional opportunities to such souls because they are metaphysically *intestate,* having made no eternal provision for their own souls by either accepting or rejecting Christ Jesus as their personal Savior. While in corporeality, some unsaved souls eventually make the decision to accept Christ Jesus as their personal Savior and eternal Lord of their life, at which moment they become *saints,* or *immortals.*

You might ask how some people who lived in Old Testament times became *Old Testament saints.* These rare souls became saints either (1) because they were completely obedient to the Will of the Creator-God or (2) because they were waiting expectantly for the prophesied Messiah to come as they sought to obey the Will of the Creator-God. Old Testament saints include, *for example:* Enoch, Abraham, Isaac, Jacob (Israel), Moses, Samuel, Elijah, and others who helped prepare for the arrival of the expected Messiah. In other words, they believed in Messiah even before Christ Jesus was born.

Discarnate souls that never become saints but are not yet demons also dwell in the dimensionless reality of Hades awaiting reentrance to the earth plane of consciousness in additional human lifetimes, or incarnations. That they will never become saints is not yet known to them although it is known to the Creator-God. He provides additional opportunities for these souls so that His final judgment and condemnation of them is justified — as well as clearly understood as justified throughout His entire creation.

Demons, devils, unclean spirits, or *evil spirits* are unequivocally known as "the eternally lost dead" or "the evil dead." The appellations in the previous sentence describe the souls of the unsaved dead who have resolutely cast their lot with Satan in rebellion against the Creator-God, having made that decision either while they were incarnates on Earth or while they were in between lifetimes (i.e., in between incarnations). Although one cannot receive salvation in between human lifetimes, one can initiate the process to become an unclean spirit if, in disobedience to the Will of the Creator-God, one refuses to reenter human form. In short, souls that become *demons, devils, unclean spirits,* or *evil spirits* make the conscious decision to eternally disobey the Will of the Creator-God.

It is because these are beyond reclamation that they are called "eternally lost." Not all of the eternally lost dead are constrained to Hell because some of them roam the earth plane of consciousness looking for human beings who are susceptible to possession, or cohabitation, by them. However, some of the eternally lost dead have already been cast out of the susceptible channels they once possessed and, therefore, are no longer able to roam the earth plane of consciousness. Instead, they are relegated to *the bottomless pit of the Abyss in Hades.*

The bottomless pit of the Abyss in Hades is analogous to a black hole in the physical universe. This bottomless pit is a dimensionless vacuum. It is the temporary abode for many of the eternally lost dead, including those who have been cast out of the earth plane of consciousness as unclean spirits.

As a side note here, the casting out of demons is either initiated by the Creator-God Himself or petitioned by a saint through the process of exorcism. For the sake of clarity, it is always the Creator-God who does the casting out regardless of who else is involved in the exorcism.

It should be noted here that *the bottomless pit of the Abyss in Hades* is temporary for three reasons: (1) It is temporary because all eternally lost dead in the bottomless pit are eventually released to terrorize human beings during *the Tribulation* as demonic locusts with scorpion-like stings (recorded as part of the first woe dispensed by the fifth angel in Chapter Nine of the Book of Revelation). (2) It is temporary because all of the eternally lost dead will eventually end up in *the Lake of Fire* throughout all eternity *(the Lake of Fire* is also known as *the second death* in Revelation 2:11, 20:6, 20:14, and 21:8). And (3) it is temporary because *the bottomless pit of the Abyss in Hades* itself is thrown into *the Lake of Fire,* along with all other levels and areas of *Hades,* at the time of the Great White Throne Judgment at the end of *the Millennium* (Revelation 20:14).

The bottomless pit of the Abyss in Hades is metaphorically and metaphysically referred to as "the sea" in certain passages of the Holy Bible. The reason that "the sea" is used to represent *the bottomless pit* is based on the humanly-understandable referent that, when one is physically floating in a large body of water, one cannot feel a floor or bottom for one's feet to touch down on. Even in contemporary modern English, *the sea* is often referred to as *the Abyss* and, as such, figuratively understood to be *bottomless*.

Here are three examples of passages in the Holy Bible that refer to exorcised demons being housed in *the bottomless pit of the Abyss in Hades* (i.e., "the sea"): (1) In Matthew 8:28-34, the demons that Christ Jesus cast out of two possessed human beings were permitted by him to enter swine who then hurled themselves into "the sea." After having been cast out by Christ Jesus, regardless of their short sojourn in swine, these unclean spirits had no place to go other than into "the sea" physically, metaphorically, and metaphysically. (2) In Revelation 9:1-3, the fifth angel, who dispenses the first of the final three woes, is given the key to the bottomless pit and, when that angel opens the pit, demons emerge as hideous locusts with scorpion-like stings to torment the unsaved on Earth for a period of five months. (Although not stated in the Holy Bible, these locust-like demons are returned to the bottomless pit at the end of those five months.) And (3) in Revelation 20:13, "the sea" gives up all of the eternally lost dead for their final judgment at the Great White Throne — at which time every one of them is vomited into *the Lake of Fire*. Hence, at the end of *the Millennium,* these demons are moved from a place of temporary torment to a place of eternal torment.

In summary, Hell (Hades or Sheol) is an incorporeal realm, or locus, of being in mortality that exists throughout the entire *Pre-Millennium* and the entire *Millennium* but does not exist in *the Post-Millennium*. Hell (Hades or Sheol) temporarily houses: (1) the souls of people who are in between incarnations; and (2) the souls of the eternally lost dead, or evil dead (also known as demons, devils, unclean spirits, and evil spirits). Many souls of the eternally lost dead are specifically incarcerated in *the bottomless pit of the Abyss in Hades* during *the Pre-Millennium,* but all souls of the eternally lost dead (except for Mohammed and the final end-time Antichrist) are incarcerated there during *the Millennium*. All demons (i.e., all eternally-damned souls) are thrown into *the Lake of Fire* at the time of the Great White Throne Judgment of the Creator-God at the end of *the Millennium*. (Mohammed and the final end-time Antichrist were thrown by Christ Jesus into *the Lake of Fire* at the beginning of *the Millennium*.)

The Lake of Fire

The Lake of Fire was vocalized, articulated, and actualized into existence by the Creator-God at the moment that the Archangel Lucifer and his angels rebelled against the Creator-God. *The Lake of Fire* exists throughout *the Pre-Millennium, the Millennium,* and *the Post-Millennium*. Although *the Lake of Fire* exists during the entire *Pre-Millennium* and the entire *Millennium, the Lake of Fire* is occupied by Satan, all fallen angels, and the souls of the eternally lost dead only during *the Post-Millennium* (except for Mohammed and the final end-time Antichrist, who were both thrown into *the Lake of Fire* by Christ Jesus at the very end of *the Pre-Millennium* — which, of course, is the very beginning of *the Millennium)*. Having just been covered in the previous section, you may recall that some souls of the eternally lost dead reside in the *bottomless pit of the Abyss in Hades* during the entire *Pre-Millennium,* and that all souls of the eternally lost dead (except for Mohammed and the final end-time Antichrist) reside there during the entire *Millennium*.

During *the Pre-Millennium,* some souls of the eternally lost dead were free to wander the earth plane of consciousness, looking to possess — that is, cohabit — the bodies of unsaved human beings susceptible to their attacks.

The phrase *the Lake of Fire* is only used in the New Testament's Book of Revelation (KJV). However, when the Hebrew word *Sheol* is used in the Old Testament, specifically in conjunction with the lowest level of hell wherein is found divine Fire, it presages *the Lake of Fire* referred to in the Book of Revelation. And, when the Greek word *Gehenna* is used in the New Testament, it often refers to, or presages, the eternal place of torment called *the Lake of Fire* in the Book of Revelation.

Except for the souls of Mohammed and the final end-time Antichrist, all other human souls condemned to eternal damnation are cast into *the Lake of Fire* at the time of the Creator-God's Great White Throne Judgment when *the Millennium* ends. For the sake of clarification, although Adolf Hitler was *an* Antichrist, he was not the final end-time Antichrist. Therefore, the soul of Adolf Hitler was not thrown into *the Lake of Fire* until the end of the seven thousand years covered by the Holy Bible. In contrast, the souls of Mohammed and the final end-time Antichrist were cast into *the Lake of Fire* one thousand years earlier than the soul of Adolf Hitler and the souls of all other eternally lost dead. Mohammed and the final end-time Antichrist were the only human souls that received such condemnation. (For proof that Mohammed is the first beast of Chapter Thirteen in the Book of Revelation, refer to Appendix C.)

The Lake of Fire is the abode of the eternally damned (i.e., Satan, his fallen angels, and his unclean spirits) and is referred to as *the second death* in Revelation 2:11, 20:6, 20:14, and 21:8. (*The first death* was covered in the section of this chapter entitled *Death.*) *The Lake of Fire* is the place of eternal torment that many people have referred to as Hell, sometimes mistakenly (if they are referring to the place that has been translated from the Greek word *Hades)* and sometimes not (if they are referring to the place that has been translated from the Greek word *Gehenna).* There are many analogous characteristics shared by *the Lake of Fire* and *Gehenna.* Unlike *Gehenna,* however, *the Lake of Fire* is a place of eternal torment and not a place of temporary torment.

The Lake of Fire is a locus in eternity and not in temporality. Hell is located in temporality and not in eternity. *The Lake of Fire* is visible to all souls in eternity. If I choose to, I can see it right now in my mind's eye (remember, I am writing to you from 3050 AD). In elaborating the parameters of *the Lake of Fire,* the God of the Holy Bible created a place of eternal torment for: (1) all demons, devils, unclean spirits, or evil spirits; (2) Mohammed and the final end-time Antichrist as well as all other antichrists; (3) the souls of all people who had the mark of the beast (i.e., the followers of Mohammed and the final end-time Antichrist); (4) all souls who openly rejected the Lord Jesus Christ as personal Savior; (5) all souls who blasphemed, insulted, or ridiculed God's Holy Spirit; (6) the fallen created being known as *Lucifer,* or *Satan;* (7) *the realm and locus of being* known as *Hades;* and (8) *the mortal state of being* known as *Death.* (To be sure, there is considerable overlap between and among many of the eight categories just listed.)

In contrast to all of the saints of the Creator-God who live during the *Post-Millennium* in a state of eternal redemption (with God in *Paradise, Heaven,* or *Eden),* the unsanctified souls of all of the eternally lost dead live in a state of eternal damnation (separated from God in *the Lake of Fire).* The souls of the eternally lost dead sought to please themselves only and, thus, joined themselves to each other in bondage to Satan, the eternal Adversary of the Creator-God, and to the fallen angels that followed Satan. The unsaved souls of the eternally lost dead chose to remain in open rebellion against the Creator-God. In contrast, the saints of God chose to be obedient to Him in their efforts to please Him.

As stated previously, in order to become an unclean spirit, a soul must make the conscious decision to: (1) always put its own will before the Will of the Creator-God, (2) always put its own desires before the desires of the Creator-God, and (3) always do what it wants to do and not what the Creator-God wants it to do.

Let me reiterate what has been covered thus far: (1) *The Lake of Fire* is a locus of being that exists in eternity. (2) *The Lake of Fire* permanently houses all created beings who recalcitrantly remained in rebellion against the Creator-God. (3) *The Lake of Fire* is in a dimensionless reality, and it is the eternal abode of the evil dead.

The truth be told, and it is being told right here, Satan never cared for any fallen being other than himself — neither any fallen angel nor any devil, demon, unclean spirit, or evil spirit. All Satan ever cared about was that all fallen beings remained loyal to him in open rebellion against the Creator-God. Joining forces with Satan in open rebellion against the Creator-God brings no special dispensation from Satan to any one of his minions. In fact, from the vantage point of eternity, all that was earned for their rebellious nature was the Creator-God's final judgment of eternal damnation and eternal torment in *the Lake of Fire*.

There are Christians in your timeframe who have rejected the notion that the Creator-God is the God of Wrath (i.e., the God of Justified Anger). They believe in universal salvation for all, including all fallen beings. Because the Creator-God is the God of *agape* love (i.e. selfless love), they have concluded that His love covers all rebellious and disobedient natures. They do not understand that, for the Creator-God to allow rebellion against Him to go unchecked and unpunished, He would be going against His own Nature.

Torment can be many things. For saved human beings, fear of divine repercussions from unconfessed sin can be tormenting. For souls who have eternally yielded to a rebellious nature, the fear of their final judgment and subsequent eternal damnation in *the Lake of Fire* is tormenting. But the pain from existing eternally in *the Lake of Fire* itself is the most tormenting of all.

Suffering in *the Lake of Fire* takes many forms for the eternally lost dead: (1) They suffer in the realization that they threw away a blissful union with the Creator-God in a communion of all saints. (2) They suffer in the realization that they influenced others to throw away their salvation. (3) They suffer by continuously re-experiencing the physical, emotional, mental, and spiritual pains that they inflicted on others. And (4) they suffer in eternal pain that is akin to the continual burning of one's flesh. (Because the eternally lost dead did not receive new somatic identities, all they each have to "wear" in *the Lake of Fire* is a likeness of their old human somatic identities.)

The Lake of Fire is horrible. You do not want to go there. Torment in *the Lake of Fire* makes brutality from human barbarism appear tame by comparison.

The Lake of Fire is compared to burning "brimstone" in Revelation 19:20, 20:10, and 21:8 because of the Fiery Nature of the living God. *Brimstone* in the New Testament is translated from the Greek word *Theion,* which is derived from *Theios. Theios* means "divinity" and *Theion* means "divine fire." When unfallen beings and restored beings are in contact with the Fiery Nature of the Creator-God, they are comforted and enlightened by it. But when the eternally lost dead are in contact with the Fiery Nature of the Creator-God, they are tormented by its unquenchable burning flame. In other words, the Fiery Nature of the Creator-God has a different effect on the two types of souls it touches (i.e., redeemed vs. damned). To be sure, because the Fiery Nature of the Creator-

God annihilates corporeality (i.e., the *shadow of death),* the Lord God Almighty rarely showed Himself to human beings without protecting them or having them protect themselves in accordance with His directions.

Because I am writing to you from 3050 AD, the following no longer exist: (1) *Hell (Hades* or *Sheol);* and (2) *Death.* Thus, the following have also ceased to exist: (1) *the bottomless pit of the Abyss in Hades;* (2) all corporeality; and (3) any incorporeality that served as a holding tank for souls who would return to Earth again in subsequent incarnations as human beings. In contrast, the following continue to exist in 3050 AD and will continue to exist throughout all eternity: (1) *Heaven, Paradise,* or *Eden;* and (2) *the Lake of Fire.* To be sure, temporality and chronological time no longer exist in 3050 AD, but unending time, spiritual time, timelessness, absolute time, and the "now" of eternity have always existed and will continue to exist.

Dimensionality

Only temporality has dimensions. Eternity is dimensionless. As a result, all created beings in eternity are dimensionless. (Because created beings in eternity have neither mass nor volume, they cannot be compacted.) Although some on Earth might say that eternity is multi-dimensional and has an infinite number of dimensions, that view would steer you in the wrong direction.

Temporality has five essential dimensions associated with corporeality: (1) length, (2) width, (3) depth, (4) time, and (5) unified spatial force. For the sake of clarification, the phrase "unified spatial force" has been coined here to include phenomena explainable through combinations of quantum mechanics, wave theory, electromagnetism, and gravity: Such a multi-pronged approach helps to explain these phenomena cohesively and coherently. Although there are some additional, obscure dimensions associated with corporeality — *for example,* dimensions related to antimatter, black holes, wormholes, white holes, and certain areas into which some subatomic particles move randomly when bombarded by other particles — the five dimensions named here are fundamental and, thus, provide a sufficient framework for at least a basic understanding of dimensionality, especially as it relates to ordinary matter.

Eternity is dimensionless as well as timeless (i.e., without solar time, lunar time, sidereal time, or atomic clock time). And eternity contains *eternal energy* (i.e., divine energy). The greatest difference between eternity and temporality is in the existence in temporality of physical mass, physical energy, and physical time and their nonexistence in eternity. (1) Metaphysically speaking, physical mass and physical energy are mathematical functions of iniquity: Because iniquity is a form of anti-*eternal energy,* when iniquity first came into contact with *eternal energy* (at the first instant that iniquity was formed), physical mass and physical energy exploded into existence at their point of contact. (2) Physical time (i.e., relative time) was also a byproduct of this explosion: Thus, metaphysically speaking, physical time is also a mathematical function of iniquity.

The primordial existence of physical mass, physical energy, and physical time actually warped *the Universe* in such a way as to bring the space-time of the physically observable universe into existence out of the explosion known to cosmologists as the *Big Bang.* Hence, temporality is the state of being where physical mass, physical energy, and physical time co-exist. (For the sake of clarification, the categories of *dark matter* and *dark energy* are also included in the physically observable universe.) Again, physical mass, physical energy, and physical time do not exist in eternity.

The concomitant events in the formation of temporality are dissected out and presented here as sequential ramifications to help make the events more understandable to the reader or listener: (1) the disobedience of created beings to the Will of their Creator formed a then-unknown metaphysical substance referred to in the Holy Bible and this book as *iniquity;* (2) *iniquity,* a type of anti-*eternal energy,* caused a vortical rift in *the Universe* as soon as it came into contact with *eternal energy;* (3) the vortical rift produced physical mass and physical energy out of the tiny bit of *eternal energy* with which iniquity first came into contact; (4) the existence of physical mass and physical energy warped the space inside of the rift, creating physical time; (5) the interaction of physical mass with physical energy caused a physical explosion (i.e., *the Big Bang)* that hurled physical mass and physical energy into space over physical time; and (6) physical mass and physical energy were hurled outward in all directions from the central point of *the Big Bang,* forming the ever-expanding physical universe over billions of years. (However, what happened over billions of years in temporality happened in a metaphysical nanosecond in eternity.)

Although the six events outlined in the previous paragraph occurred in *the Universe,* they did not occur in eternity but, rather, in an outpocketing from eternity referred to in this book as *temporality* (see Figure One in Chapter Four on page 72). Regardless of whether or not there is a multiverse including various parallel, or alternate, physical universes, the phrase *the whole Universe* in this book represents "the All" and, therefore, includes everything that exists — not just the physical universe and everything in the physical universe, but also the spiritual universe and everything in the spiritual universe. Thus, in your time (i.e., the reader's or listener's time), *the whole Universe* is composed of both eternity and temporality. In my time (3050 AD), *the whole Universe is only composed of eternity* because temporality was swallowed up, engulfed, reabsorbed, and infused by eternity at the end of *the Millennium* — after the Creator-God's Great White Throne Judgment. In the "new heaven" and "new earth," all restored created beings have learned their eternal lesson to never again create iniquity and its resulting chaos by going against the Will of the Creator-God.

To be sure, unsequestered iniquity does not exist in *the Post-Millennium* because all eternally-damned, fallen beings have been thrown into *the Lake of Fire*. That these eternally-damned beings still possess iniquity is the reason that the Lake is on fire: Their iniquity continually sparks fire as it comes in contact with the *eternal energy* that exists in the locus in which they have been sequestered. The "brimstone" of *the Lake of Fire* is actually unquenchable divine Fire.

To sequester *the Lake of Fire,* the Creator-God formed it inside a metaphysical *bubble*. Thus, *the Lake of Fire* is both inside and outside of eternity at the same time.

Following is a metaphysical reaction equation that represents the formation of temporality:

$$E^o + \bar{E}^o \rightarrow m + e^o + t = T = \Sigma D$$

where E^o is *eternal energy*, $\bar{E}^o$ is iniquity (anti-*eternal energy*),
m is physical mass, e^o is physical energy, t is physical time, T is Temporality,
and ΣD is the sum of all dimensions in the physically observable universe

The conclusion is that temporality — where physical mass, physical energy, and physical time (relative time) exist — is the sum of all dimensions in relative space-time. Therefore, *temporality* is equivalent to *dimensionality*. Corollaries include: (1) eternity does not house physical mass, physical energy, or physical time; (2)

where physical mass and physical energy do not exist, physical time does not exist; (3) where physical time does not exist, physical mass and physical energy do not exist; (4) when eternity was divided (i.e., interrupted) by iniquity, temporality resulted; (5) where iniquity exists, physical mass and physical energy also exist; (6) where physical mass and physical energy exist, physical time exists; (7) temporality houses physical time, physical mass, and physical energy; and, finally, (8) dimensionality houses physical mass, physical energy, and physical time as metaphysical functions of iniquity.

As recorded in Chapter One of the Book of Ezekiel, when eternity was opened up to the Prophet Ezekiel, he saw "a fire infolding itself" (verse 4) with "four living creatures" (verse 5), each having "four faces" (verse 6) and "four wings" (verse 6). There was a wheel (i.e., a vortex) associated with each of the four living creatures and each wheel had a wheel inside of it (verse 16). When the four creatures moved, the Prophet Ezekiel noted that the creatures did not turn in their movement. Despite the Prophet Ezekiel's existence in a multidimensional temporal world, the Creator-God permitted him to catch a glimpse of the dimensionless nature of eternity in his heavenly visions — recorded in both Chapters One and Ten of the Book of Ezekiel.

Concerning the Prophet Ezekiel's description that the living chariot of the Lord God Almighty consists of a wheel in the middle of each of the four wheels (Ezekiel 1:16 and 10:10), it might seem to the reader that he was describing the four major wheels as if each were a gyroscope. However, the Prophet Ezekiel's description of the living chariot carrying the Lord God Almighty was based on what he saw from where he was standing. In other words, it was not a mental or emotional subjectivity that caused his description to depart from how the living chariot of the Lord God Almighty actually appears in eternity but, rather, what his position was in temporality that determined his view and made his description slightly askew (i.e., askew to those of us who reside in eternity). That his description is somewhat off-center is not Ezekiel's fault. Just as where one is standing in the physical universe would result in either a geocentric view of your solar system or a heliocentric view of it, so too is the Prophet Ezekiel's description based on where he was standing and the angle of his view from temporality. To be sure, the Prophet Ezekiel saw more than the overwhelming majority of human beings have ever seen of the Creator-God and His living chariot, but Ezekiel's description of them is not as accurate as it might have been had he been viewing them from within eternity. All beings in eternity see the Creator-God and His living chariot entirely and completely — which means that we see them from every angle all at the same time: We see them from above, from below, and from every side around about all at once. This is one way that our vision in eternity is different from your vision in temporality.

Enmity

Enmity is animosity, or hostility, between the Creator-God and fallen created beings who are in open rebellion against Him. Fallen created beings who are in open rebellion against the Creator-God include: (1) Lucifer (i.e., Satan); (2) fallen angels (i.e., angels who follow Lucifer); (3) all discarnates who refuse to submit to God's Will and Authority (including unclean spirits, demons, devils, or evil spirits); and (4) human beings who reject salvation through the shed blood of Jesus Christ. Enmity exists because of the iniquity and unconfessed — and, therefore, unforgiven — sins of fallen created beings who are in open rebellion against the Creator-God. Of the four categories just listed, there is only one category in which fallen created beings still have an opportunity for salvation (i.e., redemption): Human beings who have rejected salvation through the shed blood of Jesus Christ can still be saved if they repent of their sins and accept Jesus Christ as their personal Savior, Savior of the world, *only-begotten* Son of God, and God Incarnate. Metaphysically speaking, the shed blood of Jesus Christ is the only means to repair the breach between the Creator-God and unsaved human beings. Enmity, which caused the breach, can only be dissolved through the shed blood of Jesus Christ when the efficacy of that blood is accepted in the contrition of an unsaved person.

Harboring and indulging enmity (even resentment) against another human being is practicing modern-day witchcraft. Why? Harboring and indulging enmity wishes ill upon another person in not only a spiritually unwholesome way but also in a maliciously substantive way. Metaphysically speaking, someone who is harboring and indulging enmity is in spiritual warfare against the human object of his or her enmity. Harm is visited upon the human object of enmity to the degree that the individual is susceptible to such an attack. And, paradoxically, harm is also visited upon the person who harbors and indulges enmity; in this case, the harm is experienced as spiritual, emotional, mental, and physical disequilibrium — which disequilibrium can only be healed in contrition.

Enmity was not shown in the metaphysical reaction equation given in the previous section entitled *Dimensionality* because iniquity and enmity are inseparable. They are two sides of the same coin: Where one exists, so does the other exist.

Sequence of Events

Although temporality, dimensionality, and corporeality have ceased to exist (remember, I am writing to you from 3050 AD), in eternity we can review any and all events that occurred in the physical universe from its very beginning to its very end. In order to focus on specific aspects of astronomy, geology, paleohistory, and recorded human history for the physical universe and the planet Earth, you (the reader or listener) might visit a planetarium and a museum of natural history. In eternity, we can review events that occurred anywhere in the physical universe by visiting holographic recordings of those events — which recordings are accessible in *the universal etheric theatre.*

Although each and every event that occurred in the physical universe has some relevance to the planet Earth, I will now share the timeline for those events that are the most relevant to the topics in this book:

1. (a) The Luciferian Fall and (b) *The Big Bang* [(a) and (b) are related, concomitant events] ~ approximately 14 billion years ago

2. The Origin of the Earth's Solar System ~ approximately 4.6 billion years ago

3. The Origin of Biological Life on Planet Earth ~ approximately 3.6 billion years ago

4. The Ongoing Evolution of Biological Life on Planet Earth ~ from approximately 3.6 billion years ago to the formation of "a new heaven and a new earth" (Revelation 21:1)

5. The Paleogene Extinction Event ~ approximately 66 million years ago
   [This event is significant because it removed 80% of the then-existing species on the Earth, including the massive dinosaur predators, which allowed for the successful evolution and adaptive radiation of the wide range of mammals that currently exists, including primates and modern man.]

6. The Adamic Fall ~ approximately 4000 BC
   [Although the physical bodies of *Homo sapiens* evolved, the fallen Adam and Eve materialized in human bodies when they were expelled from the Garden of Eden. The major difference between Adam and Eve and other members of *Homo sapiens* then living is that Adam and Eve and their progeny possessed souls (albeit fallen souls). All members of *Homo sapiens* without souls became extinct at the time of the Flood. All human beings after the flood had souls because they were direct descendants of Adam and Eve.]

7. The Conception of Christ Jesus ~ approximately 4 BC

8. The Birth of Christ Jesus ~ approximately 4 BC

9. The Beginning of the Earthly Ministry of Christ Jesus ~ approximately 27 AD

10. The Crucifixion of Christ Jesus ~ approximately 30 AD

11. The Bodily Resurrection of Christ Jesus ~ approximately 30 AD

12. The Bodily Ascension of Christ Jesus ~ approximately 30 AD

Specific calendar years have been assigned to the following six events to help readers conceptualize the chronological relationships of those events (numbered 13 to 18). The actual calendar years will need to be determined when the seven-year peace treaty between Israel and the final end-time Antichrist begins (see Daniel 9:27). It is the beginning of this peace treaty that triggers *the Seven Year Tribulation* and starts the countdown to the return of Christ Jesus.

13. The Seven Year Tribulation ~ estimated here as 2023 AD through 2030 AD

14. The Bodily Return of Christ Jesus (i.e., the Parousia of Christ Jesus) ~ estimated here as 2030 AD

15. Mohammed and the Final End-Time Antichrist cast into the Lake of Fire ~ estimated here as 2030 AD

16. The Battle of Gog and Magog (i.e., World War IV) ~ estimated here as 3030 AD

17. The Great White Throne Judgment of God ~ estimated here as 3030 AD

18. The Formation of a New Heaven and a New Earth ~ estimated here as 3030 AD

Chapter Six

The Relational Integrity of the Godhead

The state of being known as *mortality* is not only the effect of iniquity but also the state of sequestration for all fallen beings who themselves are iniquitous. To be sure, *the state of being* known as *mortality* is a state of sequestration for fallen beings that serves as punishment for their iniquity. The concept that iniquity is its own punishment is attested to in the Holy Bible by the multiple meanings of the Hebrew word *aw-vone'* [עָוֹן].) Indeed, it is a metaphysical irony that fallen souls punished themselves for their own iniquity by separating themselves from the Creator-God.

The entire state of being known as *mortality* is a quarantine zone, a holding tank, and an exile for created beings who have been *infected* by iniquity and must remain sequestered from the rest of God's creation. As indicated in previous chapters of this book, *the entire state of being* known as *mortality* has various realms, areas, and levels. *For example:* (1) All demons are imprisoned within the *bottomless pit of the Abyss in Hades* during *the Millennium*. And (2) all fallen souls not yet saints or demons are either (a) discarnates in mortality awaiting their next human lifetime or (b) incarnates on Earth with opportunities to become eternally redeemed. (Just as Hades is a realm in the state of being known as *mortality,* so also is corporeality a realm in that state.)

According to God's Plan of Salvation, fallen souls are consigned to mortality not only to prevent the further spread of iniquity but also to be given opportunities in corporeality to work out their own salvation in Christ Jesus or cement their individual paths to eternal damnation.

The major difference between *unsaved* fallen souls in corporeality and *saved* fallen souls in corporeality is that the unsaved do not have God's Holy Spirit residing within them. Therefore, the unsaved in corporeality do not have simple access to true spiritual understanding and are easily deceived. That is why unsaved human beings believe the best about evil people, false religion, and false prophets and the worst about good people, true religion, and true prophets. During the entire *Pre-Millennium,* there were multiple delusions that were believed by the unsaved, not the least of which was the religion of the final end-time Antichrist that was especially explosive, literally and figuratively, toward the end of *the Pre-Millennium.*

Existing in the quarantine zone of mortality even impacts saved fallen souls still in corporeality. Daily, they are faced outwardly with false evidence that appears to be real; and they are faced inwardly with the rebellious nature (i.e., carnal mind) that daily fights the divine nature they now have in Christ Jesus.

Living in a quarantine zone can even color the understanding of saved fallen souls in corporeality with regard to who and what *the Godhead* is.

As mentioned previously, *Theios* means "divinity" and *Theion* means "divine fire." The word *Godhead* is translated from *Theiotes,* and *the Godhead* includes *God the Father, God the Son,* and *God the Holy Spirit.* The Godhead, or nature of the Supreme Deity, is triune.

During *the Pre-Millennium,* all non-Christians and even many Christians did not understand how to conceptualize or describe the Godhead. They did not really comprehend in what way the one Creator-God consisted of *Father, Son,* and *Holy Spirit.* They did not understand that the Creator-God partitioned Himself into *Father, Son,* and *Holy Spirit* before the creation of the physical universe. Before the Creator-God strategized His Plan of Salvation, He was not partitioned into *Father, Son,* and *Holy Spirit.* At the end of *the Millennium,* when temporality ceases to exist, the Creator-God will, once again, no longer be partitioned into *Father, Son,* and *Holy Spirit.* Thus, the triadic partitioning of the Creator-God that you have come to know as *Father, Son,* and *Holy Spirit* only exists during *the Pre-Millennium* and *the Millennium.* (Remember, I am writing to you from 3050 AD.)

The Creator-God initiated His triadic partitioning before the beginning of temporality. (For the sake of clarity, the phraseology *before the beginning of temporality* refers to the absolute space-time in eternity and not the relative space-time in the physical universe.) The Creator-God partitioned Himself in order to effect (i.e., deploy) His Plan of Salvation for salvageable fallen souls whose iniquity caused them to become enmeshed in mortality and its temporality. The Creator-God did not need to contemplate His partitioning. He did not need to deliberate about it. He simply made it happen. The partitioning occurred in order to effect the Creator-God's Plan of Salvation, which required *God the Father, God the Son,* and *God the Holy Spirit.* After God's Great White Throne Judgment, when each unsaved soul will give an account of its actions relative to eternal redemption or eternal damnation, there will be no need for the Creator-God to continue His partitioned state. That is why *God the Father* then infuses *God the Son* at the same time that *God the Father* infuses everything over which *God the Son* had been granted power and authority (reread 1 Corinthians 15:24-28 in Chapter One on pages 29-30 or in Roundabout Number

Six of this chapter). That is also why, in the heavenly city of New Jerusalem, the Glory of God the Father and the light of the Lamb (God the Son) are indistinguishable from one another after *the Millennium:*

> And the city had no need of the sun nor of the moon to shine in it: for the glory of God did lighten it, and the Lamb is the light thereof.
>
> *Revelation 21:23 KJV Paraphrase*

Fission and *fusion* represent two important unifying concepts here. When iniquity was first introduced into *the Universe,* there was a fission of temporality from eternity. Just as the physical universe had a *Big Bang* at its origin when temporality first began, so also did the Creator-God have a *Self-determined* triadic partitioning in eternity before the beginning of temporality. Similarly, just as the mass and energy of the physical universe are restored to their original condition when the physical universe is completely infused and reabsorbed by eternity at the end of *the Millennium,* so also the Godhead's three partitions are completely reunited at the end of temporality, which is also at the end of *the Millennium.* In both sets of paired circumstances, the effects of fission are reversed by the effects of fusion at the end of temporality. To be sure, the separation of the physical universe from the spiritual universe was a type of *fission,* and the triadic partitioning of the Creator-God was also a type of *fission.* And the resorption of temporality by eternity at the end of relative space-time is a type of *fusion,* and the cessation of partitioning of the Creator-God is also a type of *fusion.*

Although the Creator-God planned everything, the Creator-God did not cause iniquity to exist. It is because the Creator-God knew that iniquity would exist that He operationalized His Plan of Salvation in accordance with *His Divine Mercy* and *His Divine*

Justice. Although the Creator-God did not create iniquity, the Creator-God decided that He would create opportunities for each soul to either choose a path to eternal redemption or remain on a path to eternal damnation. The Creator-God's ability to create includes His creation of opportunities for learning, spiritual advancement, salvation, sanctification, and reunion with Himself as well as reunion with all others who belong to Him.

>>>>><<<<<

Roundabout Number Six

The Origin of the Supreme Being's Tri-Unity

The Supreme Being has always been One and will always continue to be One. However, as recounted in Chapter One of Genesis, the Supreme Being existed as: (1) *the Lord God Almighty,* (2) *the spoken Word (the divine Logos),* and (3) *the Spirit.* Alternate titles for these three partitions include: *God the Father, God the Son,* and *God the Holy Spirit.* People who think that the Supreme Being's tri-unity is representative of three different deities are incorrect; they are using the wrong mathematical formula for their conceptualization. Instead of $1 + 1 + 1 = 3$, the correct mathematical formula to use is $1 \times 1 \times 1 = 1^3$, or one raised to the third power ($1\wedge3$). No member of this tri-unity operates independently. All three operate as One.

The earliest identification in the Bible of the tri-unity of the Supreme Being is found in Genesis, Chapter One, verses 1 through 3:

{1} In the beginning, *God* [representing *God the Father]* created the heaven and the earth. {2} And the earth became formless and void; and darkness was upon the face of the deep. And *the Spirit of God* [representing *God the Holy Spirit*] moved upon the face of the waters. {3} And *God said* [representing *God's spoken Word, the divine Logos,* or *God the Son*]: "Let there be light: and there was light."

Genesis 1:1-3 KJV Paraphrase

That *the spoken Word* in Genesis 1:3 is *God the Son* is confirmed in the Gospel According to John, Chapter One, verses 1 and 14:

{1} In the beginning was the Word *[the divine Logos]*, and the Word *[the divine Logos]* was with God, and the Word *[the divine Logos]* was God. {14} And the Word *[the divine Logos]* was made flesh, and dwelt among us, (and we beheld his glory, the glory of the *only-begotten* of the Father) full of grace and truth.

John 1:1, 14 KJV Paraphrase

Christ Jesus is also called *the Word of God* in Revelation 19:13:

And he [Christ Jesus] was clothed with a vesture dipped in blood: and his name is called *the Word of God [the divine Logos]*.

Revelation 19:13 KJV Paraphrase

The Creator-God had partitioned Himself in order to effect His Plan of Salvation for Adamic souls who would fall from immortality to mortality. The Creator-God wanted to retrieve all fallen eternal souls who would eventually repent of their waywardness in exalting themselves and, instead, return to exalting Him.

At the time of the end (after the millennial reign of Christ Jesus on Earth), when all that is to be restored to the Creator-God has been restored, *God the Father* will then infuse the Totality of His Being (i.e., *His Fiery Presence)* into the "all" that He has placed under the feet of *God the Son.* At that time, no longer will there be (1) partitions of the Supreme Being or (2) separation of the Supreme Being from His created souls — because the Creator-God will then be *All-in-all.* Although the Creator-God is "All," He is not technically "in all" until the time that Christ Jesus' millennial rule on Earth comes to an end. This infusion and reunification is attested to in 1 Corinthians, Chapter Fifteen, verses 24 through 28:

> {24} [After the millennial reign of Christ Jesus] then comes the end, when he [God the Son] shall have delivered up the Kingdom to God, even the Father; when he [God the Son] shall have put down all rule and all authority and power. {25} For he [God the Son] must reign, until He [God the Father] has put all enemies under his [God the Son's] feet. {26} The last enemy that shall be destroyed is death [mortality, corporeality, and physical death]. {27} For He [God the Father] has put all things under his [God the Son's] feet. But when he says all things are put under him [see Matthew 28:18 and John 5:26-27], it is manifest that an exception is He [God the Father] who put all things under him [God the Son]. {28} And when all things shall be subdued unto him [God the Son], then shall the Son also himself be subject unto Him [God the Father] that put all things under him [God the Son], that God [the Father] may be *All-in-all.*
>
> *1 Corinthians 15:24-28 KJV Paraphrase*

To be sure, Christ Jesus ("God the Son") already has all authority and all power in Heaven and on Earth (Matthew 28:27 and Ephesians 1:22), but not every enemy has been finally conquered yet, or "subdued unto him" (1 Corinthians 15:28). *For example,* the final end-time Antichrist will not be overcome until the end of *the Pre-Millennium.* And *death* — not just physical death but the entire state of being known as *mortality* — will not be expunged from *the whole Universe* until the end of *the Millennium.*

End of Roundabout Number Six

>>>>><<<<<

The Tri-Unity of God

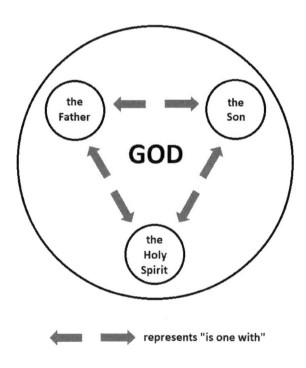

⟸ ⟹ represents "is one with"

From "The Threeness of God" (page 76)

©2021 by Rev. Joseph Adam Pearson, Ph.D.

www.christevangelicalbibleinstitute.com/English3.pdf

Chapter Seven

Metaphysical Intervention

Metaphysics is a branch of philosophy as well as a branch of theology. *Metaphysics* is the study of unseen realities. As a branch of philosophy, *metaphysics* is the study of intellectual realities. As a branch of theology, *metaphysics* is the study of spiritual realities. (Intellectual and spiritual realities are both *unseen*.)

Theological metaphysics includes studying the nature, or essence, of the highest spiritual reality that thoughts are things and things are thoughts. It also takes into account that there is a spiritual universe in addition to a physical universe. If it is well-balanced, it does not negate that there is a physical universe. Instead, it takes into consideration that there is a higher spiritual reality of which an understanding is necessary in order to effect a change in various human conditions. Sometimes, students and practitioners of *theological metaphysics* employ spiritual truth in seeking to effect emotional, mental, physical, spiritual, and/or social change. To be sure, *Christian metaphysics* is the highest form of *theological metaphysics*.

In Chapter Four, I mentioned that "attempting to *speak things into existence* by human beings is mostly a sign of gross spiritual immaturity." I mentioned it because there are a few different camps of spiritual thought that misuse the truth about employing spiritual verities to effect change in emotional, mental, physical, spiritual, and social conditions. In such camps, the truth is not misused to an evil end. It is misused in ignorance to an ineffective and, sometimes, harmful end. People who misuse the truth of effecting change by spiritual means include: (1) people who misconclude that they are the original source of power and authority; (2) people who think subconsciously that the Creator-God can be controlled; (3) people who think that, if you declare what you wish to be true, it should come true and will eventually come true; (4) people who do not factor the Will of the Creator-God anywhere into the spiritual equations or formulas they are employing; and (5) people who think it is alright to demand change from the Creator-God in the guise of "working with Him" rather than "working under Him."

In order to effect change in human conditions, people must actually *walk* in the Will of the Creator-God, recognizing that there are *always* mitigating factors related to the Will of the Creator-God that are neither seen nor understood. In other words, people become presumptive about the spiritual truth they think they know and, as a result, end up insulting the Creator-God. When you insult the Creator-God, you distance yourself from Him and dampen the efficacy of His truth in your life. (For the sake of clarity, God does not distance Himself from you; you distance yourself from Him.) Unless you move in humility, recognizing that only the Creator-God knows everything, you will never be able to utilize spiritual truth in order to effect change in any human condition. In other words, have faith, but do not take anything for granted.

For the people who subscribe to a "name it, claim it" or a "confess it, possess it" theology, Christ Jesus stated: "If you abide in me, and my words abide in you, you shall ask what you will, and it shall be done unto you" (John 15:7 KJV Paraphrase). In order for the naming and claiming (or confessing and possessing) to work, you must be abiding in Christ Jesus not just by saying that you are but by living ethically and morally in humility, mercy, and truth. You also must not be afraid of your own shadow. You must be courageous in speaking the truth as well as speaking about the truth. And you must not think that your own words have more power than they actually do. Otherwise, you might become unhinged or unbalanced because of your presumptions.

Proper application of John 15:7 to human conditions requires spiritual maturity as one seeks the Will of the Lord. The truth of John 15:7 cannot be denied, but the maturity of many claiming its truth can be denied. Many claim its truth without ever inquiring of the Lord what His Will is concerning a specific human condition or the reasons why the condition exists, persists, and does not change despite naming and claiming (or confessing and possessing) its change.

Saying that it is a lack of faith that hinders change when naming and claiming the change is not always accurate. Sometimes the lack of change is a better fit with God's Will in His broader plan for (1) an individual, (2) a group of individuals, or (3) groups of individuals.

Christ Jesus also said: "Abide in me, and I in you. Just as the branch cannot bear fruit of itself unless it abides in the vine, no more can you bear fruit unless you abide in me" (John 15:4 KJV Paraphrase) and "Whoever does the Will of God abides forever" (1 John 2:17b KJV Paraphrase).

The most important point here is that, if the student of the Holy Bible is misusing or misapplying the truth of John 15:7, then (1) the Will of the Lord and (2) naming and claiming a change for a human condition will not be in synch with one another. *For example,* those who subscribe to a "name it and claim it" or a "confess it and possess it" theology sometimes think they can impose their human will on the Lord God Almighty, manipulate

Him to do what they want, control Him with the right spoken formula, or even demand that He honor His written Word (as they understand it) without ever inquiring of the Lord God Almighty what His thinking is concerning a specific situation or condition.

Accepting that the Will of the Creator-God supersedes naming and claiming a change, or confessing and possessing a change, is the spiritually mature position that does not lead others astray with *a one-formula-fits-all* interpretation of Scripture.

If you were to seek a national leader's permission to accomplish something, you would approach the leader humbly and courteously. Even if the leader gave you the permission or the authority to do something, you would still take into consideration: (1) in what ways you might please the leader and (2) in what ways you might displease the leader. To be sure, you would want to monitor yourself to make sure that you were walking in the will of the leader (i.e., doing things according to the way the leader would want them done). These principles should also be applied to seeking the Will of the Creator-God in attempting to metaphysically change the specific human conditions of (1) an individual, (2) a group of individuals, or (3) groups of individuals.

In order to effect change in a human condition, you can ask the Creator-God to intercede or intervene at the same time that you ask that the requested change be in keeping with His Will; and you can affirm the goodness of the Creator-God as you visualize the change taking place at the same time that you ask that the visualized change be in keeping with His Will. Both methods combined (supplication and metaphysical affirmation) are underutilized by everyone. But correctly affirming the truth is underutilized more than supplication because people understand less about affirming the truth and how to apply truth metaphysically.

Naming and claiming change, or confessing and possessing change, in a human condition is not the same as metaphysically affirming the truth to effect change. Naming and claiming a change fancies itself as *working with* the Creator-God; however, metaphysical affirmation of the truth acknowledges *working under* the supervision of the Sovereign Lord God Almighty. Although subtle, *working with* does not show the same respect as *working under*. Yes, one day you will be working as joint heirs *with* the Lord Jesus Christ, but that day does not come until you have fully joined him in eternity.

When the truth sinks in, you (the reader or listener) should have a prevailing emotion. The prevailing emotion should be remorse for being insulting and disrespectful to your Creator. How have you been insulting and disrespectful to Him? You do not consult Him. You do not ask Him if your understanding of His truth is correct and applicable to the particular situation at hand. You underestimate your Creator. You misconclude that your Creator does not know best. You fail to acknowledge the omnipotence and omniscience of your Creator. You try to manipulate your Creator. And you are not mindful of your Creator's feelings (i.e., His emotions). In your remorse, you should apologize to your Creator for offending Him by being presumptive. (Indeed, presumption is a form of arrogance.) You should ask for His forgiveness. And you should commit yourself to seek His Will at the same time that you commit yourself to live in a state of perpetual contrition.

How can you evaluate the authenticity of someone to whom you might go for help to effect change in human conditions through spiritual means? Generally speaking, if someone tells you that they are a prophet, disbelieve them. A true prophet will *never* tell someone that they are a prophet. If someone tells you that they are a spiritual healer, disbelieve them. Someone who is a spiritual healer will *never* proclaim that they are. If someone tells you that they can communicate with people in Heaven, disbelieve them. Someone who actually communicates with saints in Heaven will *never* announce that they can. People who are spiritually gifted in any of these areas will demonstrate their gifts naturally and effortlessly as the Creator-God creates opportunities for them to do so and leads them to others who might benefit from the operation of their gifts. Authentically-gifted people who are walking in the Will of the Creator-God will *never* try to promote themselves. And they will *never* seek praise or honor from other people. Instead, they will ask that all praise and all honor go to the Lord God Almighty.

If the truth be told (and it is being told in this book), prayer itself employs principles of metaphysics. How? By using words to create a petition, people are using symbols of a higher truth. Words themselves may capsulize the truth, but the words only represent the truth. They are not the truth-in-itself. What actually makes them the truth? Belief, or faith, that the Creator-God is who He said He is as recorded in the Holy Bible; and belief, or faith, that the Lord Jesus Christ is who he said he is as recorded in the Holy Bible. Without belief, or faith, backing them up, the words you might use in a prayer mean absolutely nothing. They only mean something and, therefore, carry weight when you believe what you know — and know what you believe — about the Creator-God. To be sure, what you believe about the Creator-God must be as accurate as it can be given your level of intellect and level of spiritual maturity (no one on Earth knows everything all at once and our Creator-God factors that in as He evaluates your requests and responds to them).

Earlier, in Chapter One, I introduced you to the concept of an "authentic Christian." Here, I introduce you to the concept of an "authentic Jesus." An "authentic Jesus" is not who you say he is or what non-Christian books say he is; an "authentic Jesus" is what he himself says he is and what the Holy Bible says he is. So, you must not only strive to be an *authentic Christian,* you must also strive to know the *authentic Jesus*. Those who choose to rely on what they have learned from non-Christian belief systems, or what they have concluded about Jesus without studying the Holy Bible, show that they do not love the truth and prefer delusion to the truth. Unless they reverse themselves, they guarantee their eternal damnation:

> {10b} They refused the love of the truth that they might be saved. {11} And, for this cause, God shall send them strong delusion, that they should believe a lie: {12} That they all might be damned who did not believe the truth but have pleasure in unrighteousness.
>
> *2 Thessalonians 2:10b-12 KJV Paraphrase*

There are different shades of iniquity and different categories of sin that can impede the efficacy of: (1) prayers to the Creator-God and (2) metaphysical affirmations of who you and others are in Christ Jesus. Just because you may not have the necessary means to fulfill your iniquitous and sinful desires does not mean that these desires will not impede your prayers or your metaphysical affirmations. *For example,* just because you have not committed adultery when there was no opportunity for you to do so is no reason to rejoice, especially if you harbor the desire to commit adultery (however unfulfilled it may be). That is why it is so important for you to know yourself — meaning, your inadequacies, infirmities, vulnerabilities, and propensities to sin. And that is why living in a state of perpetual contrition is so very important to: (1) your relationship with the Creator-God, (2) effectual prayer, and (3) effectual metaphysical affirmation. Living in a state of perpetual contrition acknowledges to the Creator-God that you know you will be flawed for as long as you remain in a corporeal state — at the same time that you ask for forgiveness from the Creator-God for your inadequacies, infirmities, vulnerabilities, and propensities to sin. As you stand firm in your understanding of the power and authority of the shed blood of Jesus Christ, you are employing *Christian metaphysics. Standing firm in the shed blood* is neither literal nor figurative. *Standing firm in the shed blood* is metaphysical. *Standing firm in the shed blood* is metaphysical because it is faith-based. (It would be figurative only if it were used in a poetic sense by someone who is merely offering lip service to its truth or is blithely commenting about it.)

Metaphysical affirmations include: (1) using words as symbols, and (2) using visualized imagery to project a desired effect. Concerning your own physical health or the physical health of someone else you know, you do not need to have an extensive knowledge of human anatomy and physiology (i.e., how the human body is constructed and how its various levels of organization function and interrelate), but the more you know the better for the corrective application of metaphysical affirmations in verbalization and imagery for a physical problem. There are those who might say that, the more you understand human anatomy and physiology, the more you are impeded from effecting a change because your faith-based belief system will be undermined by your lending credence to a reality that is physical. That is simply not true. The Creator-God may honor someone's prayers despite that person's unknowing ignorance, but He will not honor someone's prayer request if that person's ignorance is chosen or if that person revels in his or her own ignorance. Similarly, the Creator-God may honor someone's metaphysical affirmations despite that person's unknowing ignorance of (1) human anatomy and physiology or (2) a specialist's medical diagnosis, but, again, He will not honor someone's affirmation if that person's ignorance is chosen or if that person revels in his or her own ignorance.

Both prayer and metaphysical affirmation utilize the *eternal energy,* or *divine Fire,* of the Godhead. In Greek, *Theios* means "divinity," *Theiotes* means "Godhead," and *Theion* means "divine fire," or "the *eternal energy* of the Creator-God." I will now introduce a useful neologistic paradigm for you to use. A *neologism* is "a newly-devised word or a new sense to an already existing word." And a *paradigm* is "a model, pattern, or framework useful in explaining something." The word that I now introduce to you in its singular form is *theion* (its English plural form is *theions*). For the purpose of this communication, a *theion* is "the smallest indivisible unit of divine, or eternal, energy." (This definition satisfies the "new sense" aspect of a *neologism*.) An analogy that might help your understanding is: "a *theion* is to divine energy and divine light as a *photon* is to physical energy and physical light." Just as a *photon* is a force-carrying, massless elementary particle in the physical universe, so is a *theion* a force-carrying, massless elementary particle in the spiritual universe.

Using *divine energy* (i.e., *eternal energy*) for spiritual, or metaphysical, healing is akin to utilizing little packets of spiritual energy to create beneficial healing radiation. In the physical universe, harnessing photons to generate useful energy can be achieved by using an energy funnel to concentrate the photons. In the spiritual universe, harnessing *theions* to generate healing radiation can be achieved by using one's faith in Jesus Christ as Lord and Savior to concentrate the *theions*. One's belief in Jesus Christ as Lord and Savior permits one to focus divine energy, or *theions,* on an area that is problematic in order to resolve the condition metaphysically through vocalized and/or visualized affirmations of the desired effect. For the sake of clarification, laying hands on the person to be healed can augment the focus, but laying hands on the person to be healed is not required for a successful Christian metaphysical treatment.

One measure of the utility of the photon to *theion* comparison is in the capacity of the units to self-replicate or not. Because photons are not able to self-replicate and *theions* are able to self-replicate, the photon to *theion* comparison is less than perfect. However, it is still a useful analogy, and conceptualizing *theions* provides a practical paradigm for Christian metaphysicians in the practice of their faith.

The reason that *theions* are able to self-replicate is that they are made of divine Love in addition to divine Light. (In the metaphysical reality of God, divine Light and divine Love are inseparable.) The Creator-God Himself is composed of *theions*. Thus, His very nature, or essence, includes the quality of His desire to self-replicate — or, in this case, create beings in His complete image and perfect likeness. To be sure, this desire is born of His divine Love. His divine Love desires to be shared with others in fellowship, communication, compassion, tenderness, mercy, grace, and care. Because the Creator-God *is* divine Love, He wants (no, *needs)* to share the largess of it with others, specifically by creating beings in His complete image and perfect likeness.

The only danger in utilizing the *theion* paradigm is in a misguided conclusion that you can know the unknowable or can reduce the omnipotent, omniscient, and omnipresent Creator-God to your own limited terms of understanding. What guards against operating in this misguided conclusion is your ability to live in a state of perpetual contrition, which state is against the fallen nature of being human but very much a part of the restored nature of being divine by being recast in the complete image and perfect likeness of the Creator-God through the shed blood of Jesus Christ, His *only-begotten* Son.

You should not expect anything to turn out well if you go against the Holy Spirit, the-One-who-can-Help. Here, *the-One-who-can-Help* refers to the Holy Spirit Himself as well as to someone used by the Holy Spirit to help on His behalf through the spiritual gift of "helps" (1 Corinthians 12:28 KJV). God's Holy Spirit is your Teacher, Advocate, Encourager, Comforter, and Helper

(John 14:16, 14:26, 15:26, and 16:7), but God's Holy Spirit sometimes chooses another person (i.e., someone other than yourself) to act as your teacher, advocate, encourager, comforter, and helper on His behalf. If you are walking in the Will of the Creator-God, you can expect God's Holy Spirit to help by answering prayer and responding to metaphysical affirmation. Help from God's Holy Spirit is your bloodright through the sacrificial atonement of Christ Jesus. However, when you step outside of the Will of the Creator-God, you mar the path of the Lord God Almighty — meaning, you obstruct the help and blessings He intends for you. Thus, when you obstruct the path of the Holy Spirit, He cannot help you. The Holy Spirit "cannot help you" not because He is weak and ineffective but because He does not honor prideful obstinacy and arrogance. In being prideful and obstinate, you put up your own barriers to the blessings of the Creator-God through the help, or aid, of His Holy Spirit, *the Helper.*

Chapter Eight

Where are You?

The most important question that you can ever answer is: "Where are you positionally relative to the cross of Jesus Christ?" Subsumed within that question are the following three questions: (1) What is your theological position on and about the cross of Jesus Christ? (2) Of what significance is the cross of Jesus Christ to your own life? (3) Where are you metaphysically in relationship to the cross of Jesus Christ?

(1) What is your theological position on and about the cross of Jesus Christ?

All human thinking and coping skills are dependent on where you are theologically relative to the cross of Jesus Christ. If you do not have the right theological position, or are not on the road to the right theological position, then your reasoning is bound to be off-kilter and clouded. Any and all further elevation of your thinking and coping skills is dependent on where you are theologically relative to the cross of Jesus Christ.

Here is a figurative analogy that might help: It is as if you are currently living on the top floor of a skyscraper. You may have come to the misconclusion that you cannot advance to any higher level because you are on the skyscraper's uppermost floor (i.e., you are limited to your current understanding of who Jesus Christ is). However, you discover that you can go higher by adding floors to the skyscraper (i.e., by increasing your knowledge of who Jesus Christ is). But adding floors to the skyscraper can only be achieved by extending yourself into the empty space above the uppermost floor (i.e., into the dimensionless reality of eternity). Such a stretch can only be accomplished through the planks in the scaffolding that you will use to build additional floors (i.e., the planks of your understanding who Jesus Christ is through comprehensive, long-standing Bible study). In other words, the planks and scaffolding needed to construct additional floors require your fully understanding the person, personality, and role of Jesus Christ relative to *the whole Universe* through comprehensive, long-standing Bible study accompanied by prayer and meditation.

During your lifetime, *the whole Universe* consists of both temporality and eternity (remember, people are either reading or listening to this book during *the Pre-Millennium* or *the Millennium)*. In 3050 AD, *the whole Universe* consists only of eternity because temporality has ceased to exist. "Death, or mortality, was swallowed up in victory by Life" at the end of *the Millennium* (1 Corinthians 15:54c combined with 2 Corinthians 5:4c). Therefore, because you are still living in temporality, you must be brought to an accurate understanding of the person, personality, and role of Jesus Christ not only in temporality but also in eternity.

What is the role of Jesus Christ in eternity and in temporality? Before temporality, dimensionality, mortality, and corporeality began, Jesus Christ existed within the one Godhead but not in the person of Jesus Christ. What the Holy Bible calls: (1) the Lord God Almighty, (2) Jesus Christ, and (3) God's Holy Spirit were indivisible and unpartitioned from one another before the beginning of temporality. (As stated in Chapter Six, the phrase "before the beginning of temporality" refers to the absolute space-time in eternity and not the relative space-time in the physical universe.)

The three components of the Godhead were not just figuratively *united* or metaphysically *one* before the beginning of the physical universe. They were indistinguishable from one another. Simply stated, there were no distinctions in the Godhead relative to God the Father, God the Son, and God the Holy Spirit before the beginning of temporality. (Please reread Roundabout Number Six in Chapter Six of this book.)

What is triune during *the Pre-Millennium* and *the Millennium* did not exist as triune before the beginning of temporality. Before the beginning of temporality, the three existed inseparably as one. In other words, there was no "three" before the beginning that is referenced in Genesis 1:1 (i.e., "In the beginning..."). However, in order to effect His Plan of Salvation for souls who would fall because of iniquity and sin (i.e., the Adamic Fall), the Godhead partitioned Himself before He began to create order from the chaos caused by the Luciferian Fall. To effect His Plan of Salvation, the Creator-God partitioned Himself into: (1) Yahweh (the Lord God Almighty); (2) the divine Logos (the spoken Word or articulated Principle of God); and (3) the Ruach HaKodesh (the Holy Spirit of God). All three are evidenced in Chapter One of Genesis: (1) the Lord God Almighty in Genesis 1:1, (2) God's Holy Spirit in Genesis 1:2, and (3) God's spoken Word (the divine Logos) in Genesis 1:3. Later, in temporality, the divine Logos would become known as Jesus Christ, who is the full embodiment of the Creator-God in human flesh as the Creator-God's *only-begotten* Son (i.e., God Incarnate).

Yahweh sent His *only-begotten* Son to Earth to redeem unsaved souls in corporeality. Yahweh declared that anyone in corporeality who would accept Jesus Christ as the Creator-God's *only-begotten* Son and only Savior of the world — and would accept the blood that he shed on the cross of his crucifixion as the only payment acceptable to Yahweh for iniquity and sin — would not be eternally damned but, instead, be eternally redeemed. After his crucifixion, murder, resurrection, and ascension, Jesus Christ entered his destiny as Sovereign over heaven and Earth (Matthew 28:18) until the end of temporality, when he would present a fully-yielded creation to Yahweh for Yahweh's complete infusion by His Fiery Presence (such infusion occurring at the end of *the Millennium*).

Many people do not understand the concept of *only-begotten*. For some readers of the Holy Bible, their lack of understanding comes in their confusing Adam as "the son of God" (Luke 3:38 KJV) with Jesus Christ as "the *only-begotten* Son of God." Yes, Adam was the son of God, but Adam was not the *only-begotten* Son of God. Depending on your perspective, Adam was created by God either *ex nihilo* (i.e., out of nothing) or *de novo* (i.e., out of unformed matter). But Jesus Christ was *begotten* by the Creator-God in consort with a human mother. Adam was not born of a woman, but Jesus Christ was born of a woman. Mary provided the egg and the Creator-God created the sperm for the conception of Jesus Christ. The Lord God Almighty did not create Jesus Christ *ex nihilo* or *de novo* within Mary's uterus. And, regardless of how the Lord God Almighty created the spermatozoon that fertilized Mary's egg, Mary's egg was not created *ex nihilo, de novo,* or through the manipulation of Mary's chromosomes. Both Mary and the Creator-God were equal contributors to the conception of the physical body of Jesus Christ. They each contributed 23 chromosomes to that body's conception. Mary was the mother of Christ Jesus and the Lord God Almighty was the Father of Christ Jesus. Thus, Jesus Christ is *the only-begotten Son of God, a son of Adam* and *King David* (i.e., a descendant of Adam as well as King David), and *God-in-flesh* (i.e., God Incarnate). Through His Holy Spirit, the power of the Creator-

God overshadowed Mary for her impregnation at the time that Jesus Christ was conceived (Luke 1:35).

> Whoever shall confess that Jesus is the Son of God, God dwells in that person, and that person dwells in God.
> *1 John 4:15 KJV Paraphrase*

> The person who overcomes the world is the person who believes that Jesus is the Son of God.
> *1 John 5:5 KJV Paraphrase*

> The person that has the Son has life, but the person that does not have the Son of God does not have life.
> *1 John 5:12 KJV Paraphrase*

There are also those whose misunderstanding of the Holy Bible causes them to misconclude that, although Jesus Christ is the "begotten" Son of God, Jesus Christ is not the *only* "begotten" Son of God. Because they mistakenly believe that the following verses are referring to King David, they have misconcluded that King David was also "begotten."

> {6} "Yet have I set My king upon My holy hill of Zion."
> {7} The Lord God Almighty said unto me: "You are my Son; this day have I *begotten* you. {8} Ask of Me, and I shall give you the heathen [the Gentile nations] for your inheritance, and the uttermost parts of the Earth for your possession."
> *Psalm 2:6-8 KJV Paraphrase*

Psalm 2:6-8 is prophetic scripture. In Psalm 2:6, the God of the Holy Bible is not speaking of King David but of the *King of kings,* Jesus Christ. The "King" in Psalm 2:6 is Jesus Christ. Thus, the *begotten* in Psalm 2:7 is Jesus Christ. This reference in Psalm 2 to Jesus Christ is confirmed in multiple locations in the New Testament that quote Psalm 2:7:

> God has fulfilled the same promise unto us in that he has raised up Jesus again; as it is also written in the second psalm: "You are My Son, this day have I begotten you."
>
> *Acts 13:33 KJV Paraphrase*

> For unto which of the angels said God at any time: "You are My Son, this day have I begotten you"? or "I will be to him a Father, and he shall be to Me a Son"?
>
> *Hebrews 1:5 KJV Paraphrase*

> So also Christ glorified not himself to be made a high priest but it was God who said unto him: "You are My Son, today have I begotten you."
>
> *Hebrews 5:5 KJV Paraphrase*

Many people do not understand the word *begotten* as used in the Holy Bible. The first man Adam was not *begotten* by the Creator-God. King David was not *begotten* by the Creator-God. Only Jesus Christ was *begotten* by the Creator-God. *Begat* means that the Creator-God Himself provided the sperm, or seed, and that Mary herself provided the egg for Jesus to be born. Mary was an equal contributor to the conception of Jesus Christ's physical body and not just an incubator, oven, or petri dish for the development of a person who was created *ex nihilo* or *de novo*. Jesus Christ was not just born "from" a virgin or created "inside" a virgin, Jesus Christ was born "of" a virgin (i.e., Mary was his biological mother). Jesus Christ was not half-human (i.e., half of a descendant of Adam) and half-God (i.e., half of a descendant of God). Jesus Christ was fully human, and Jesus Christ was fully God. In this way, Jesus Christ is the only *begotten* Son of God the Father. Jesus Christ was the most unique person who ever lived. No other person was *begotten* of the God of the Holy Bible. No other person will ever be *begotten* of the God of the Holy Bible in the same way that Jesus Christ was *begotten*.

Psalm 2:6-8 is prophetic Scripture about the Savior, Jesus Christ. It states clearly in Psalm 2:8: "Ask me, and I will make the heathen your inheritance, and the ends of the Earth your possession." The Hebrew word for "the heathen" (or "the nations" in other translations) is "goyim," which means "the Gentiles." King David did not rule over the Gentile nations throughout the whole world (i.e., to "the ends of the Earth"). King David was only the local king of the children of Israel in the land of Israel. Only the Savior of the world, Jesus Christ, rules over the Gentile nations throughout the whole world as Head of the Christian Body (i.e., the Church Universal).

In order to be theologically accurate, you cannot just believe that Jesus Christ existed. You must believe that Jesus Christ is the *only-begotten* Son of God as well as God Incarnate. This belief is what divides the sheep from the goats, the saved from the unsaved, and immortals from mortals.

> For God so loved the world that he gave his *only-begotten* Son that whoever believes in him should not perish but have everlasting life.
>
> *John 3:16 KJV Paraphrase*

> The person who believes on him is not condemned: but the person who does not believe on him is condemned already, because that person has not believed in the name of the *only-begotten* Son of God.
>
> *John 3:18 KJV Paraphrase*

In this was manifested the love of God toward us because God sent his *only-begotten* Son into the world that we might live through him.

1 John 4:9 KJV Paraphrase

Whoever does not believe that Jesus Christ is the *only-begotten* Son of God while he or she is in corporeality remains unsaved and condemned to eternal damnation. Unfortunately, recognizing the truth that Jesus Christ is the *only-begotten* Son of God while one is in incorporeality as a discarnate does not bring one to salvation and eternal redemption. The decree of the Lord God Almighty is that we must accept Jesus Christ while we are in human flesh (i.e., in corporeality) in order to receive His gift of eternal redemption.

(2) Of what significance is the cross of Jesus Christ to your own life?

Knowing Jesus Christ theologically does not mean that you know Jesus Christ personally. In order to know Jesus Christ personally, you must have an intimate relationship with him. You begin having an intimate relationship with Jesus Christ when you not only understand who he is theologically but also who you are in him, by him, through him, and for him. You must arrive at the point where you attribute your life and everything good that you have in it to Jesus Christ.

You must walk with him continually. You must talk with him continually. You must share with him who you are. You must share with him what pleases you, and you must share with him what displeases you as well. You must seek to honor only him, and you must seek to honor him by pleasing him. You must seek to be a righteous holy man or a righteous holy woman. Everything must revolve around him. Although he is already the metaphysical center of *the whole Universe,* he must become, and remain, not only the center but also the circumference of *your* personal universe.

Eventually, you must come to the understanding that Jesus Christ is your greatest reward and that you already possess your greatest reward as a saved created being.

Your heart's desire must be to please him in all that you do, say, think, and feel. You must learn to reject all unethical, immoral, and unwholesome thinking. You must learn to embrace the truth about yourself and your unclean desires and be willing to change your approach to life. No change can come about without the innermost and uttermost desire of your soul to please him. No mental change. No emotional change. No physical change. No metaphysical change. No spiritual change. Nothing happens without him. Even the strength to endure your earthly challenges, burdens, aging, sickness, disease, disadvantages, disabilities, and inabilities comes solely from him.

You need to acknowledge him not only as Savior of the world but also as your own personal Savior. And not only Savior but also your Sovereign (i.e., Lord), brother, friend, covenant partner, provider, rewarder, blesser, comforter, nurturer, actualizer, and the very reason for living, moving, and being. And you must be willing to sacrifice your life daily as well as be willing to be murdered for your faith in Jesus Christ (of course, without presumptively or purposely placing yourself in harm's way).

The Holy Bible is clear that Jesus Christ is *the living Word of God,* or *the divine Logos*. John 1:1 states: "In the beginning was the Word *[the divine Logos]*, and the Word *[the divine Logos]* was with God, and the Word *[the divine Logos]* was God." In completing the answer to the second question, it is important to note here that some Christians who know that *the Logos* is God Incarnate are embarrassed to admit: (1) that Jesus Christ is also the *only-begotten* Son of God, (2) that the *only-begotten* Son of God audibly spoke to his heavenly Father, and (3) that his heavenly Father audibly spoke to him. They are embarrassed to admit these three truths because these truths are at odds with their denominational or personal theology. Indeed, there is a flaw in their theology. They have warped *the utterances of God (the rhema word of God)* in order to prove their misguided point about *the living Word of God, the divine Logos.* Though they claim to be *full gospel,* they really are not *full gospel.* You may fellowship with these people without subscribing to their way of thinking. It is they who are deficient in their ability to conceptualize the Creator-God as triune, not you.

3) Where are you metaphysically in relationship to the cross of Jesus Christ? (And to what extent are you being changed through the cross of Jesus Christ?)

This question pertains to your changing position as measured in the timeless and dimensionless state of eternity. Indeed, you are either *for* Christ or *against* Christ, but it goes much further than that for those who are *for* Christ and still in human bodies. Such people are measured in eternity according to their actions: (1) on behalf of Christ, (2) because of Christ, and (3) for Christ.

Your actions in corporeality are categorized in eternity as:

ethical (a) or unethical (a⁻)

moral (b) or immoral (b⁻)

forgiving (c) or unforgiving (c⁻)

loving (d) or unloving (d⁻)

hospitable (e) or inhospitable (e⁻)

discerning (f) or delusional (f⁻)

helpful (g) or hurtful (g⁻)

edifying (h) or destructive (h⁻)

Although the eight sets of opposing actions presented in the previous list are measured in the timeless and dimensionless state of eternity, perhaps the figurative, dimensional representation that immediately follows might help you to more easily conceive of how they are measured:

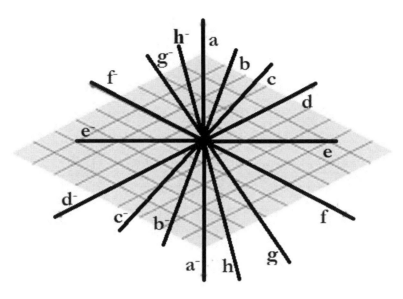

Figure Two

In Figure Two, each of the eight sets of opposing actions are on a sliding scale, or continuum. *For example,* if discerning actions (f) are based on truth and delusional actions (f⁻) are based on error, the more actions based on spiritual discernment that you perform will move you into the positive side of the continuum for that set. In other words, where you are on the f/f⁻ continuum is based on the mean of all of your actions with regard to that category. The greater the mean for each set of opposing actions, the closer you are metaphysically to the cross of Christ for that particular category. The grand mean (i.e., the mean of the means for all eight categories) determines your overall metaphysical position in relationship to the cross of Christ. In other words, the closer you are metaphysically to the cross of Christ, the more you are emulating him in your own daily walk by being ethical, moral, forgiving, loving, hospitable, discerning, helpful, and edifying. Because the

Creator-God is omniscient, omnipotent, and omnipresent, none of these eight categories are actually calculated, reckoned, or derived by Him: They are simply known by Him for each person in corporeality. And, for the sake of clarity here, the Creator-God does *not* give mathematical scores to saved human beings. All of this, of course, will be much clearer to you during your life review, which occurs after you step into eternity at the end of your human life.

The schematic of Figure Two is only the present author's overly-academic attempt to help readers conceptualize categories in which they are evaluated by God. As I see it, the merit in sharing these sets of opposing actions is in helping you: (1) to evaluate your own actions in each category to see if you need to change; and (2) to determine if there might be additional sets of opposing actions that could be included in the paradigm.

To help you do your homework, let us take an example of *loving* (d) versus *unloving* (d⁻) actions relative to the three main questions posed in this chapter. (1) Understanding love in action *theologically* requires that we recognize that Jesus Christ gave the ultimate sacrifice of love for us all on his cross at Calvary. (2) Understanding love in action *personally* requires that we recognize the significance of the love of Jesus Christ to our own salvation, sanctification, eternal redemption, and overall well-being. And (3) understanding love in action *metaphysically* requires us: (a) to monitor and evaluate our own thinking, feeling, words, and behaviors in relation to keeping or not keeping a record of having been wronged by others; (b) to recognize that this is how we are being evaluated by the Creator-God; and (c) to understand that the more we are not keeping a record of others' wrongs against us, the closer we are to Jesus Christ himself and the more intimate our relationship is with him while we are in corporeality.

Appendix A

Reincarnation and the Holy Bible

I.

Reincarnation is the reentrance of unsaved fallen souls into corporeality as human beings. Although concepts of reincarnation are elaborated in at least some forms of Zoroastrianism, Hinduism, Buddhism, and Judaism, there is a dearth of systematic theology in Christianity associated with reincarnation. The major objections to reincarnation by Christian theologians include, but are not limited to, the ideas that: (1) reincarnation seems to negate the need for Christian salvation; and (2) reincarnation seems to confuse the Biblical notion of the resurrection of the human body. Although other objections exist, the two just mentioned are the most substantive.

In response to the two objections just posed: (1) Reincarnation does not negate the need for Christian salvation if one simply views reincarnation as the multiple opportunities for salvation that the Creator-God gives errant souls, which opportunities provide additional evidence of His unparalleled grace, mercy, and justice. (2) Reincarnation does not confuse the Biblical standard of the resurrection of the human body if one understands that, at the time of Jesus Christ's return (his Second Advent), the somatic identity of the Christian believer is: either (a) reconstituted from the dust of a decomposed physical body into an *astral gelatinous*™ form (i.e., a spiritual body) in the case of a saint who is already with Christ Jesus in Paradise at the time of Christ Jesus' return to Earth; or (b) translated from a living physical body into an *astral gelatinous*™ form (i.e., a spiritual body) in the case of a saint who is in corporeality (i.e., still alive in a human body) at the time of Christ Jesus' return. (See Roundabout Number Two in Chapter One of this book for an explanation of the phrase *astral gelatinous*™).

II.

Most Biblical Christians flatly reject reincarnation because the Holy Bible does not introduce it as a construct for a Judeo-Christian systematic theology. Perhaps the most damning Bible passage used against reincarnation is found in the Epistle to the Hebrews:

> {27} As it is appointed unto men once to die, and after this the judgment, {28} so also was Christ offered once to bear the sins of many; and to those who look for him shall he appear the second time without sin unto salvation.
>
> *Hebrews 9:27-28 KJV Paraphrase*

Biblical Christians fail to recognize the possibility that Hebrews 9:27 is referring to all souls collectively suffering *spiritual death* (i.e., spiritual mortality) at the same time in their original separation from the Creator-God due to their iniquity and sin in the Adamic Fall. (*Adam* is not only the name of an individual who lived approximately 4,000 years before Christ Jesus but also a plural Hebrew noun that represents created Adamic beings in the collective sense.) The present author's point is that one could interpret Hebrews 9:27 as follows: "it is appointed to all souls collectively to die once [i.e., *be separated from the Creator-God once]"* and not "it is appointed to a soul to experience only one human death."

To be sure, it is not appointed to all souls collectively to *die twice* in the Biblical sense because only those souls who have irrefutably rejected Jesus Christ as their personal Savior are *twice dead* (Jude 1:12 KJV); the second death of eternally damned souls occurs when they are thrown into *the Lake of Fire* at the end of *the Millennium.* (Remember, the Lake of Fire is also known as *the second death.*) In other words, the collective fall of all souls at the same time may be referred to as *the first death,* and *the first death* is not referring to the death of an individual human being. Seen in this light, *the first death* (i.e., spiritual mortality, or separation from the Creator-God) was appointed to all souls at the same time because of the collective iniquity and sin of humankind from the Adamic Fall.

For the sake of clarity, *the first death* is entirely different from *the second death:* (1) *The second death* is not referring to reincarnation. And (2) *the second death* is not appointed to all souls but, rather, only to those souls who have irrefutably rejected Jesus Christ as: (1) the *only-begotten* Son of the Creator-God, (2) God Incarnate, (3) the promised Messiah of Israel, and (4) their Personal Savior. References to *the second death* are found in the Book of Revelation in the following verses:

> Those who have an ear, let them hear what the Spirit says to the churches: the person who overcomes [through faith in Christ Jesus] shall not be hurt of *the second death.*
>
> *Revelation 2:11 KJV Paraphrase*

> [Including saints martyred during *the Tribulation:*] Blessed and holy is the person who is part of the first resurrection: on such *the second death* has no power, but they shall be priests of the Creator-God and of

Christ and shall reign with him a thousand years.
Revelation 20:6 KJV Paraphrase

{14} And death and hell were cast into *the Lake of Fire*. This is *the second death*. {15} And whoever was not found written in the Book of Life was cast into *the Lake of Fire.*
Revelation 20:14-15 KJV Paraphrase

But the fearful, and unbelieving, and abominable, and murderers, and whoremongers, and sorcerers [including drug dealers], and idolaters, and all liars [including apostates and heretics], shall have their part in the lake that burns with fire and brimstone, which is *the second death.*
Revelation 21:8 KJV Paraphrase

To summarize at this juncture: this short discussion of *the first death* and *the second death* is intended to clarify their meanings in order to help the reader understand that the two phrases are not referring to the reincarnation of individuals but, instead, to the collective separation of individuals from the Creator-God — temporary separation in the case of *the first death* and permanent separation in the case of *the second death.*

III.

Reincarnation cultists are often self-driven to prove that reincarnation is mentioned in the Holy Bible. Unfortunately, their so-called proof is speculative, revisionist, and specious. Because they neither understand nor respect the authority of the Holy Bible, reincarnation cultists often invent places in Scripture that supposedly refer to reincarnation. *For example,* they might incorrectly use specific Bible verses like Matthew 11:13-14, Matthew 17:10-13, and Mark 9:11-13 to "prove" that John the Baptist was a reincarnation of the Old Testament Prophet Elijah.

Reincarnation cultists also try to revise history to help support their position that the earliest Christian Church embraced reincarnation. To be sure, one notable figure in the early Christian Church, Origen Adamantius (182 - 254 AD), believed in reincarnation, but his views on this topic were considered heretical by the majority of his contemporaries.

The Holy Bible does not refer to reincarnation. However, just because the Holy Bible does not refer to reincarnation does not mean that reincarnation does not exist. Similarly, just because the Holy Bible does not refer to electricity does not mean that electricity does not exist. There are those who will say that statements supportive of reincarnation cannot be true because (1) such statements would be contradictory to the Holy Bible and (2) the Creator-God does not contradict Himself. To be sure, the Creator-God does not contradict Himself. However, as presented here, reincarnation is not really contradictory to any truth in the Holy Bible. Rather, an intelligent understanding of reincarnation helps us to explain certain gaps in understanding spiritual truth concerning people who have died never having heard the gospel message of Jesus Christ while they were on Earth. The only way that reincarnation would be contradictory to the truth in the Holy Bible is if it were used to replace the need for the shed blood of the *only-begotten* Son of God as the sole means for salvation. But I am advocating that you reject any such erroneous assertion.

The Apostle John heard and saw many truths, but he was not permitted to record all of them for others to know:

When the seven thunders had uttered their voices, I was about to write: and I heard a voice from heaven saying unto me: "Seal up those things which the seven thunders uttered, and do not write them."

Revelation 10:4 KJV Paraphrase

Revelation 10:4 illustrates that, although the Holy Bible contains everything that human beings really need to know for one's salvation and sanctification, the Holy Bible does not contain every single spiritual truth or fact. The present author is not trying to suggest here that the concept of reincarnation was revealed by the Creator-God to the Apostle John in Revelation 10:4. He is merely stating that there are some truths and facts that are neither recorded nor represented in the Holy Bible.

Certainly, an understanding or belief in reincarnation was never, is not now, and will never be required for the salvation and sanctification of one's soul. Unfortunately, in many instances, a superficial understanding of reincarnation distracts souls from their real purpose. That is one reason that the construct of reincarnation was not introduced in the Holy Bible. Another reason is that the primary focus of the Holy Bible is the deliverance and salvation of the Creator-God's chosen people through faith in the God of the Holy Bible alone and not postponing salvation for some speculated future incarnation.

IV.

Heaping their grief — that is, widening their separation from the Creator-God — some reincarnation cultists espouse the transmigration of souls from one biological species to another. Although human beings are animals *(Homo sapiens),* they are the only creatures that: (1) have souls made in the image and likeness of the Creator-God, (2) possess elevated consciousness (i.e., a higher order awareness of who they are), and (3) are free-will agents who make moral decisions. Souls are *not* appointed by the Creator-God to inhabit any earthly creature other than the human creature. To be sure, Christ Jesus did cast out unclean spirits (i.e., the souls of demonic discarnates) from a possessed man and gave them permission to enter the bodies of nearby swine (Matthew 8:28-33; Mark 5:1-13; Luke 8:27-33). However, the transmigration of human souls to other animals, including pigs, does not occur as part of the Creator-God's plan for salvation, spiritual development, and spiritual advancement.

V.

Reincarnation is meant for the purpose of a soul's spiritual development and advancement; it is not meant for the purpose of a soul's retrogression and/or devolution. If the ember of the Creator-God's *Life* is not rekindled in a soul during its sojourn on Earth, then the soul simply turns into another human creature at the time that it reincarnates. This, of course, does not happen if the soul refuses to re-enter corporeality. Then, the soul becomes an unclean spirit, demon, devil, or evil spirit (all four terms are used synonymously throughout the various versions and translations of the Holy Bible).

Reincarnation plays a major role in the pattern of the Creator-God's Justice. It provides opportunities for fallen souls to progress in spiritual awareness so that they can eventually make an informed decision concerning their acceptance or rejection of Jesus Christ as Lord, Personal Savior, and Sovereign King.

Without an understanding of: (1) salvation only through Christ Jesus and (2) sanctification only by the Creator-God's Holy Spirit, reincarnation cultists have both romanticized reincarnation and inflated it to the position of an end in itself rather than the means to an end.

The most important moment in each soul's existence is the one in which it either completely accepts or completely rejects Jesus Christ as Personal Savior. After that moment, the most important moment is the one that is occurring right now and not in some distant past incarnation or some imagined future incarnation.

Disclaimer

The incarnation of the Creator-God as Jesus Christ is not to be confused with reincarnation. Likewise, references to the pre-incarnate Christ and the post-incarnate Christ are not to be confused with reincarnation. The *only-begotten* Son of the Creator-God existed before "the Word (or Logos) was made flesh" (John 1:14, KJV) — just as he continues to exist today as the Risen Christ in his post-incarnate state. Jesus Christ did not need to progress spiritually in order to become *the Christ* (the promised Messiah of Israel) and Savior of the world. Why? Jesus Christ is not only the *only-begotten* Son of God the Father, Jesus Christ *is* Deity as part of the triune God (Colossians 2:9).

Appendix B

A Glossary of Terms

Abyss: the bottomless pit in Hades: (1) to which some fallen angels and exorcised demons have been cast during *the Pre-Millennium;* and (2) to which all fallen angels and all demons are temporarily incarcerated during *the Millennium*

astral gelatinous™: the nature of the primal living substance composing the somatic identities of: (1) all unfallen created beings in eternity; and (2) all restored living beings in eternity after *the Millennium;* the type of spiritual substance of immortal beings that has translucent, luminescent, and iridescent spiritual qualities; used synonymously by the present author with *metacrystalline, supracrystalline, supraplasmic,* and *glorified*

chronological time: relative time measured from solar, lunar, sidereal, and atomic clock calculations; physical time (in contrast to spiritual time); time in temporality

corporeality: *the shadow of death; the shadow of turning;* the realm of mortality in which souls inhabit human bodies; the physically-visible realm of mortality; the physical condition, mode, or realm of being in mortality; physicality; corporeal mortality

death: the condition of mortality separating fallen created beings from the Creator-God; the state of being also called *mortality* ("the first death")

Eden: see *Heaven*

eternity: the unsequestered state where the Creator-God, His unfallen angels, and His restored saints live, move, and have their being; the timeless and dimensionless state of the true creation of God; the spiritual universe; absolute time

glory: the spiritual *brightness*, or *luminosity*, of God that is a quality of the spiritual supramolecules (i.e., theions) of His Sovereign and Supreme Being; eternal energy; divine Light; living Fire

Hades: *Hell* or *Sheol;* the realm and locus where incorporeal mortal beings exist during *the Pre-Millennium* and *the Millennium;* although *Hades* is an incorporeal condition, mode, or realm in the state of mortality, it is considered a part of temporality because its existence is of a specified — and, therefore, *temporal* — duration

Heaven: the eternal state of glorious being for the Creator-God, His unfallen creation, and His restored creation; also known as *Paradise* and *Eden*

Hell: see *Hades*

immortality: the state of being in eternity for: (1) unfallen created beings and (2) restored created beings who had once been unsaved and fallen but are now saved and eternally redeemed

immortals: immortal beings; *elohim* (as used in Hebrew in Psalm 82:6 and quoted by Christ Jesus in John 10:34); a category that includes: (1) all unfallen beings in eternity and (2) all beings in eternity and temporality whose souls have been saved by the Lord Jesus Christ

incorporeality: an invisible realm of mortality and an invisible realm of immortality; a condition, or mode, of being in which souls do not inhabit human bodies; the nonmaterial condition of: (1) all discarnate souls in the state of mortality as well as (2) all discarnate souls in *Heaven;* incorporeal mortality

iniquity: the turning of created beings away from the Creator-God in disobedience and rebelliousness; the spiritually-substantive effect of such a turning; a metaphysical substance that explosively reacts with eternal, or divine, energy; anti-*eternal energy* (a useful analogy is: anti-*eternal energy* is to *eternal energy* as antimatter is to matter)

Lake of Fire: the sequestered state and locus of being to which Lucifer, all fallen angels, and all unsaved souls have been assigned; the state of eternal damnation that houses all eternally-damned beings after *the Millennium;* the place of eternal torment; also known as *the second death;* because it is in a metaphysical *bubble, the Lake of Fire* is both inside and outside of eternity

metaphysician: a metaphysical practitioner of Christian truth; one who applies spiritual truths to identify, resolve, and correct problems associated with the human condition

metaphysics: a division of philosophy and theology that describes and/or employs the nature of unseen realities; the true essence and meaning of things as thoughts and thoughts as things

Millennium: the 1,000 year period during which Christ Jesus reigns on Earth

mortality: the state of being for souls who fell from eternity because of their iniquity; *the first death; Death*

mortals: mortal beings; unsaved fallen beings that are either in corporeality as incarnates or in incorporeality as discarnates

Paradise: see *Heaven*

Post-Millennium: the period in eternity after the formation of "a new heaven and a new earth"

Pre-Millennium: the 6,000 year period from the time of the human Adam and Eve to the time that Christ Jesus returns to Earth at the beginning of *the Millennium*

saints: souls living temporarily in corporeality or permanently in eternity who have yielded their own individual wills to the Will of the Creator-God; saved souls (including saved souls in corporeality as incarnates and saved souls in *Heaven* as discarnates)

Sheol: see *Hades*

sin: any action based on iniquity

temporality: the condition of relative time that exists in corporeality as measured by solar, sidereal, lunar, and atomic clock calculations

theion: a neologism representing the smallest indivisible unit of eternal energy that is composed entirely of divine Light and divine Love (for the sake of clarity, *divine Light* and *divine Love* are inseparable)

Tribulation: the final seven years of *the Pre-Millennium;* the seven years that immediately precede the return of Christ Jesus to Earth at his *Second Advent,* or *Parousia*

unclean spirits: the discarnate souls of the eternally-damned; the evil dead; also known as *evil spirits, demons,* and *devils*

Universe (i.e., *the whole Universe*): includes everything that exists; during *the Pre-Millennium* and *the Millennium, the whole Universe* includes everything that exists in temporality as well as everything that exists in eternity; in *the Post-Millennium, the whole Universe* includes only those things that exist in eternity because temporality has ceased to exist

Appendix C

Proof that Mohammed represents the First Beast in Revelation, Chapter Thirteen

The simplest phonetic transcription of "Mohammed" is:

(1)   M   O   H   A   M   E   D

In ancient Hebrew, the closest counterparts of these sounds are:

(2) Mem Waw Hey Aleph Mem Yod Dalet

The proper character representation for "Mohammed" in John's vision is:

(3)   ם   ו   ה   א   מ   י   ד

Note: The Apostle John thought, understood, and "saw" in Hebrew, which is written from right to left. However, the backward cipher transcribes this Hebrew word from left to right. Thus, the so-called "final Mem" (the representation of Mem when it ends a Hebrew word) is used in the beginning place here.

In Hebrew, the numerical equivalents of the characters above are, respectively:

(4)   600   6   5   1   40   10   4

(5) The sum of the above numbers is 666, or "Six hundred threescore and six" (Revelation 13:18 KJV).

Books By The Author

As I See It: The Nature of Reality by God by Rev. Joseph Adam Pearson, Ph.D., Christ Evangelical Bible Institute, Copyright 2022. ISBN 978-0615590615.

Classroom Version of As I See It: The Nature of Reality by God by Rev. Joseph Adam Pearson, Ph.D., Christ Evangelical Bible Institute, Copyright 2021. ISBN-13: 978-1734294705.

God, Our Universal Self: A Primer for Future Christian Metaphysics by Rev. Joseph Adam Pearson, Ph.D., Christ Evangelical Bible Institute, Copyright 2020. ISBN 978-0985772857.

Divine Metaphysics of Human Anatomy by Rev. Joseph Adam Pearson, Ph.D., Christ Evangelical Bible Institute, Copyright 2022. ISBN 978-0985772819.

Hello from 3050 AD! by Rev. Joseph Adam Pearson, Ph.D., Christ Evangelical Bible Institute, Copyright 2022. ISBN 978-0996222402.

Christianity and Homosexuality Reconciled: New Thinking for a New Millennium! by Rev. Joseph Adam Pearson, Ph.D., Christ Evangelical Bible Institute, Copyright 2021. ISBN 978-0985772888.

The Koran (al-Qur'an): Testimony of Antichrist by Rev. Joseph Adam Pearson, Ph.D., Christ Evangelical Bible Institute, Copyright 2020. ISBN 978-0985772833.

Telugu Version of Quran: Testimony of Antichrist by Rev. Joseph Adam Pearson, Ph.D., Christ Evangelical Bible Institute, Copyright 2020. ISBN 978-0996222457.

Urdu Version of Quran: Testimony of Antichrist by Rev. Joseph Adam Pearson, Ph.D., Christ Evangelical Bible Institute, Copyright 2021. ISBN 978-0996222440.

Revelation of Antichrist by Rev. Joseph Adam Pearson, Ph.D., Christ Evangelical Bible Institute, Copyright 2021. ISBN 9780996222488.

Intelligent Evolution by Rev. Joseph Adam Pearson, Ph.D., Christ Evangelical Bible Institute, Copyright 2022. ISBN 978-0996222426.

The Biology of Psychism from a Christian Perspective by Rev. Joseph Adam Pearson, Ph.D., Christ Evangelical Bible Institute, Copyright 2020. ISBN 978-0996222464.

The Threeness of God by Rev. Joseph Adam Pearson, Ph.D., Christ Evangelical Bible Institute, Copyright 2022. ISBN 978-1734294729.

About The Author

Dr. Joseph Adam Pearson is a college and university educator with more than fifty years of classroom and administrative experience. Dr. Pearson has been the International President and Chief Executive Officer of Christ Evangelical Bible Institute (CEBI) for over twenty-five years. At the time of the publication of the latest edition of this book (2022), he still oversees thriving branch campuses of CEBI in India, Pakistan, and Tanzania.

Currently, Dr. Pearson spends the majority of his time developing, designing, and deploying curriculum for Christian education nationally and internationally. And he preaches, teaches, and leads international crusades as well as provides group pastoral training in global mission settings.

During his professional life, Dr. Pearson has also served in the role of Senior Pastor of Healing Waters Ministries in Tempe, Arizona and as Dean of Instruction for Mesa Community College in Mesa, Arizona — where he was founding instructional dean for its Red Mountain Campus as well as Director of its Extended Campus.

Dr. Pearson believes that after we are saved, and at the same time that we are being sanctified, our individual actions are part of an "application" for the jobs that we will each perform during Christ Jesus' Millennial reign on Earth. Dr. Pearson's greatest goal is to be one of the many committed Christian educators who will be teaching during that period of time.

You may contact the author at

drjpearson@aol.com

or

drjosephadampearson@gmail.com

Visit the author's legacy web sites at

www.dr-joseph-adam-pearson.com

and

www.christevangelicalbibleinstitute.com

Made in the USA
Columbia, SC
05 October 2022

68344742R00096